Praise for *No One Taught Me How to Be a Man*

"I wish I could have read *No One Taught Me How to Be a Man* when I was young. I've read plenty of books about masculinity (and gender in general) over the years, and this is one of the best. It's not only an insightful reflection on gender; it is a wise and perceptive exploration about living consciously and compassionately."

—Carl McColman, author of *Eternal Heart* and *Read the Bible like a Mystic*

"In a world where men are actively discouraged from reflecting on what it means to be a man, this smart, highly readable invitation to do so from someone who clearly has is urgently needed. With meaningful personal anecdotes and an approach that speaks to all varieties of men (and anyone who has ever cared about one), *No One Taught Me How to Be a Man* is an essential book."

—Chris Stedman, author of *IRL* and *Faitheist*, and writer and host of Unread

"*No One Taught Me How to Be a Man* is a much-needed book for men of all sorts. In this book, Shannon T. L. Kearns offers a vision for what a positive, progressive masculinity could look like and invites us all to join in the conversation, whether we are queer or straight, cisgender or transgender, stereotypically masculine or charting our course."

—Brian G. Murphy, author of *Love beyond Monogamy* and *Reading the Bible through Queer Eyes*

"Desperately needed in our current conversations about gender is a deeper understanding of healthy masculinity. In *No One Taught Me How to Be a Man,* Shannon T. L. Kearns helps us to understand the social, cultural, and religious pressures men face from a trans man's point of view. Poignant and thoughtful, this book is a lifeline for those lost in the noise of contemporary ideas about masculinity."

—Kaya Oakes, author of *Not So Sorry* and *The Defiant Middle*

"In a culture where conversations about masculinity often vacillate between simple answers and dismissals of the crisis afflicting men, *No One Taught Me How to Be a Man* brings desperately needed nuance. It's a courageous book that treats the way patriarchy harms men with tenderness and compassion, while still centering the harm it does to others. Not content with naming what is wrong, Kearns offers a path out. And as someone whose own masculinity has often been a site of pain and dysphoria, I didn't just find this book engaging. I found it healing."

—Rev. Benjamin Perry, author of *Learning to Cry*

"In a time of divisive culture wars, Shannon T. L. Kearns invites us to a nuanced conversation about gender and masculinity. Leading the way with courage and compassion, he presents an expansive vision for men that encourages them to live into authenticity and wholeness. This is a must-read for those wanting to explore masculinity when the old narratives of toxic patriarchy no longer work."

—Cait West, author of *Rift: A Memoir of Breaking Away from Christian Patriarchy*

"Kearns recounts his transition into masculinity with candor and authenticity, revealing the complexities hidden in our assumptions about what masculinity is and is not, while also asking poignant questions along the way. At once an inquiry into traditional notions of cisgender masculinity, a roadmap for change, and an analysis of how we might be able to inhabit healthier, more inclusive masculinities, *No One Taught Me How to Be a Man* shows us that if destructive notions of manhood can be learned, they can also be unlearned—if we're willing to do the work."

—Timothy J. Hillegonds, author of *The Distance Between*

No One Taught Me
How to Be a Man

NO ONE TAUGHT ME HOW TO BE A MAN

SHANNON T. L. KEARNS

What a Trans Man's Experience Reveals about Masculinity

BROADLEAF BOOKS
MINNEAPOLIS

NO ONE TAUGHT ME HOW TO BE A MAN
What a Trans Man's Experience Reveals about Masculinity

Copyright © 2025 Shannon T. L. Kearns. Published in association with The Bindery Agency, www.TheBinderyAgency.com. Published by Broadleaf Books. All rights reserved. Except for brief quotations in critical articles or reviews, no part of this book may be reproduced in any manner without prior written permission from the publisher. Email copyright@broadleafbooks.com or write to Permissions, Broadleaf Books, PO Box 1209, Minneapolis, MN 55440-1209.

30 29 28 27 26 25 24   1 2 3 4 5 6 7 8 9

Library of Congress Cataloging-in-Publication Data
Names: Kearns, Shannon T. L., author.
Title: No one taught me how to be a man : what a trans man's experience
   reveals about masculinity / by Shannon T.L. Kearns.
Description: Minneapolis : Broadleaf Books, 2025. | Includes
   bibliographical references.
Identifiers: LCCN 2024023628 | ISBN 9798889830924 (hardback) | ISBN
   9798889830931 (ebook)
Subjects: LCSH: Masculinity. | Transgender men. | Kearns, Shannon T. L.,
Classification: LCC BF692.5 .K43 2025 | DDC 155.3/32—dc23/
   eng/20240801
LC record available at https://lccn.loc.gov/2024023628

Cover collage by Gabe Nansen
Cover design by Gabe Nansen

Print ISBN: 979-8-8898-3092-4
eBook ISBN: 979-8-8898-3093-1

Printed in China.

To my trans brothers—
we remake the world by being ourselves.

Contents

Acknowledgments

To Ashley for seeing me, for loving me, for building a life with me.

To Adam for always being in my corner, for deep conversations and deep laughter, and for being the kind of friend people long for. I'm so lucky to call you mine.

To Brian for all we've built together and all we continue to build and for your deep friendship every step of the way.

To the Turbos crew for welcoming us into your lives and your community and becoming our chosen family.

To the Transmasculine Community Network circa 2008 for teaching me about community.

To Trinity McFadden and the entire team at the Bindery for caring so much and supporting my work and writing.

To Andrew DeYoung for making this book better: for deepening my thinking, challenging me, and being an excellent conversation partner.

To the team at Broadleaf: Adrienne Samuels, Doreen Michleski, and others who so diligently and passionately work to make books better and get them in the hands of readers.

Thank you to the Banff Centre for Arts and Creativity and to the Ucross Foundation for space and time to go deeply into this project and for taking such good care of artists.

Introduction

When I posted online that I was writing a book about masculinity, someone commented, "I'm sorry. You have nothing to add to this topic." When you hear that I'm a transgender man, you might agree with that random internet commenter. As a trans man, my credentials might seem, to some, to be suspect, yet it's this very identity that has helped me see and understand masculinity in a new way. As a transgender man, no one taught me how to be a man. I wasn't raised as a man, nor was I indoctrinated into masculine spaces. When I figured out my own maleness (after a lifetime of wordless *not-enoughness*), I had to make a masculine space for myself.

My sense, from talking with many other men and extensively studying the research on masculinity, is that even those who were raised as men feel they, too, had to figure it out on their own. This struggle to figure out what it means to be a man and how to feel like you're enough gets more complex as the world changes rapidly. We continue to look for models to help us sort out how to be in the world.

As I tried to figure out what being a man meant to me, I went first to the various streams of conversations about men and masculinity, but in each of them, I found something to be lacking. Some fundamental piece was missing. There were resonances, but none of them fully explained my experience of the world. Some were centered on body parts, and I knew from experience that it wasn't those parts that made me a man. Some were centered on healing relationships with other men, but I had close male friends, and that wasn't doing it either. Some were focused solely on how to get and maintain relationships with women, and that, too, felt like not the whole picture. Something was missing.

I did what many men try to do: I experimented. I tried on lots of different ways to be a man—from the hyper-masculine man, to the fierce protector, to the gentleman—until finding some kind of mix that felt authentic and didn't do harm to the people around me. On that journey, I looked to other men, to media portrayals of masculinity, to feminist conversations about toxic masculinity, and in each place, I tried to figure out where I fit and what was missing.

I realized that my unique upbringing, my own journey, and what I've experienced in moving through masculine spaces might help unlock something for men who have the same sense that something is missing but can't quite figure out what.

You might be wondering why we need another book about masculinity. Haven't we spent enough time talking about men and men's issues? On the surface, it certainly seems men have been centered in far too many conversations for far too long, and the spate of books about the various crises in masculinity seem designed to make that center hold. And yet, in the midst of all of the conversations, we seem to have found very few solutions.

Talking about masculinity isn't new. While there haven't been the same well-defined waves as there have been in the feminist movement, there have definitely been streams of conversation that overlap, argue with one another, and try to solve the problem of masculinity. In this work, the questions often become: Is it masculinity that's the problem or is it men? Is it possible to separate the two? Is there a way to encourage healthy masculinity? And what happens if we disagree on what healthy masculinity means?

People have posited all sorts of solutions to the issue: Some thinkers say if we could simply recover some kind of warrior ethos, we'll be all right. Others say we just need kinder and gentler men. Some have theorized that it's about connecting with an absent father or healing your father wound. Others want us to engage in initiation rites often stolen from Indigenous communities. There are some who believe the way forward is to eradicate gender entirely. Some say everything masculine is toxic, while others say toxic masculinity doesn't exist and people are just shaming men for being men. What's often lost in the midst of these schools of thought is the average man just trying to get through the day—men who feel like they are floundering and don't know where to turn for help. From my conversations with other men, many of us feel like something is missing. Something isn't right. We feel like there should be more, but we have no idea how to get it. We continually feel like we're not measuring up to what our partners want and are expecting, to the other men in our lives, to a society that seems to keep moving the goalposts.

It feels like hyperbole, but when we look at the statistics, there is, indeed, a crisis in masculinity. This isn't some far-right talking point about how we need to "man up," nor is it simply a liberal left viewpoint about eradicating all of gender. No, this is a real crisis that is threatening the health, relationships, and well-being of men. And because of the way many men have been raised and indoctrinated, when men are hurting, they tend to hurt the people around them. All you have to do to see that this threat is real is look at the data: from men delaying going to the doctor, to men having few to no friends outside of their romantic partners, to the high rates of suicide. Not only that, but men are also struggling with how to parent, how to date and find partners, and how to connect. These statistics affect not only men but also everyone in those men's lives. There are direct links between the ways men are suffering and the harm they do to other people. If we truly want a healthy society, we have to address this crisis. What we've been doing hasn't been working. We need a new kind of thinking and intervention that will allow men to show up for themselves and others.

This book is an examination of masculinity that isn't centered on biology or body parts. It's an exploration of what it might take to be a good man in this world that seems filled with toxic men. It's about masculinity that centers women and other people of marginalized genders but that also makes space for men to be themselves. It's a plea for a healthy masculinity, a wholehearted masculinity, and a gentle masculinity. And it's written by a man who had to figure out on his own what masculinity was.

This book is for men. If you identify as a man, if you move through the world as a man, then you are welcome here. We're not going to define what makes a man in this book. I don't care what body parts you do or don't have. I don't care who you're attracted to or not attracted to. I'm not worried about your testosterone level or your chromosomes or your DNA. If you are a man, this book is for you. If you're wondering if you're "man enough," you are. If you're wondering if I'm going to try to tell you to stop being a man, I'm not. If you're wondering if I'm going to prescribe a one-size-fits-all version of masculinity (that once again leaves you out), then fear not and keep on reading.

This book *won't* argue that there's only one way to be a man and that trans men, queer men, and anyone who doesn't fit the stereotype aren't men. Nor will it say that masculinity is just fine and the real problem is all the women getting so upset about things. I don't think the way forward is to reclaim the past and bring back old notions of chivalry and manliness.

If you're open to the conversation, then let's have it. If you're hungry to think about being a man in new ways, if you're feeling lonely in your masculinity, if you're feeling like there's no room for you in the world anymore, this book is for you. If you're feeling like all of the old ways are dying out, and you just don't understand why, then read on. If you're wondering why it seems like so many men are dying by their own hands or struggling to form relationships or feeling isolated, then we're in this together. If you're a trans man who's trying to figure out how to inhabit your new identity, if you're a queer man who senses you've got some unhealthy practices or coping skills to unlearn, if you're still figuring out what masculinity means to you, you'll find a place here.

What we're not going to do in this book is decide who gets to be a man and who doesn't. That's a losing game for all of us. It sets up walls, and you might be surprised to find yourself on the outside of them. For too long, this idea of "one right way to be a man" has left too many of us feeling like we're not enough. We're not tough enough or cool enough or strong enough. But on the other hand, there are men who feel like they're not sensitive enough or quiet enough or gentle enough to fit in anymore. This book is for all of us as we try to figure out what it means to be men in our current world.

I'm not going to ask you to stop being a man. I'm not going to tell you that we need to abolish gender or get rid of the binary, but I am going to ask what we mean by *masculinity*. I am going to invite a conversation about how we're showing up as men and if that's actually serving us. I want us to open the doors to the secret places where many of us are wrestling but are afraid to say it out loud.

Yes, we'll talk about how to be better husbands and fathers, but in some ways, that's a side note. It will happen automatically if we learn to be healthier men. If we learn to be healthier men, our relationships (all of them—friendships too) will deepen. Our physical health will get better. Our mental and spiritual health will improve. We'll see a shift in our relationship to ourselves and our communities. Does that seem miraculous? I promise it's possible. If we show up. If we do the work. If we allow ourselves to ask the questions and really listen to the answers and change the ones that we don't like.

This book is inclusive of transgender men (obviously, as it's written by one), and it's inclusive of men who are gay or queer and of men who are straight and who have never questioned either their gender or their sexuality a day in their lives. Our experiences of masculinity will differ from each other based on our class, our race and ethnicity, and the ways we were raised. Instead of trying to flatten the experience of masculinity, we should open it up. We all have something to learn from one another.

It's no secret the world is changing, and many of us are feeling left behind. The jobs that were once highly coveted for their security, longevity, and high pay don't exist anymore, and they're not coming back. The ways many of us were taught to be, to speak, to act, to treat others aren't seen in the same light anymore. The ways we formed relationships in the past aren't available to us. In a world of fast and easy connection, we are lonelier than ever before.

After years of struggling, exploring, and experimenting, I've come to an experience of masculinity that I dream of for all men. I want us to have ease in our bodies; to feel like we are enough; to have solid partnerships; to feel capable and competent in our workplaces and in our households; to have deep friendships; to be physically, mentally, and spiritually healthy; and to be content. While this might sound like a far-fetched dream, I do believe it's possible.

Make no mistake—it will take courage. Courage to go against the grain. Courage to face our deepest selves. Courage to shift generational narratives. When we do these things, people will push back. It will be uncomfortable (for us and others). We'll have to learn new ways of being and speaking and hold tight to them even as it disrupts those around us. Change is hard. It's easier to just keep doing what we've been doing even if it doesn't work anymore.

We need courage now more than ever. Courage to face what's no longer working for us. Courage to shake off ways of being that are holding us back. Courage to lean into discomfort and take charge of our growth so we can be the people we want to be.

Here's what I promise: it will be worth it.

CHAPTER ONE

Suffering in Silence

It feels hard to talk about being a man. At the same time, it feels hard to watch men continue in crisis (and often feel we're causing it ourselves). There is something so fraught in talking about gender, something so intimate to so many of us. Any critique can feel like a weapon, especially if there are places we're feeling our needs are going unmet.

It can sometimes feel like we're putting up a shield so we can protect ourselves, but we can't talk about that because it would make us seem too vulnerable. That feels dangerous, too. We hide behind jokes and sports and disconnection as we try to figure out what it means to be men in today's world.

My experiences of masculinity (like the experiences of all men) are inseparable from culture, from my family of origin, from media, and yes, from hormones and biology too. How do we talk about masculinity without smoothing it over and making it all one thing when we all know it isn't? At the same time, how do we honestly confront what isn't working in us and for us while also making space to be honest about the places we suffer?

Part of my journey has been having to get honest with myself about my own failings while also getting honest about the places that hurt. I've had to realize the places in my life where I could easily fall into thoughts and actions that are unhelpful for me or for others. Yet it's often been my experiences as a transgender man that have *kept* me from engaging in harmful behavior. By sharing my experiences with you, I'm hoping to provide a model that breaks us out of unhealthy patterns and allows us more freedom while also acknowledging the harm we can do and changing those behaviors.

Whenever I give a talk about trans identity, I usually offer a joke: "If I had been born a cisgender man, I'd be an asshole!" It never fails to get a laugh, but it's also true. I grew up in a culture that prioritized men and where I had gifts and skills that had I been born a cisgender man, would have been uplifted and honored. Those same skills, in a body presumed to be female, were looked at askance. I had to fight to find and keep my voice, fight to develop my leadership, and fight to find my place. Had I been a cisgender man, I wouldn't have had to fight, and that lack of fighting, I believe, would have made me grow up to be an asshole or, at the very least, a bit entitled. I would have grown up oblivious to the challenges faced by women, oblivious to what it means to make space for other people, and not at all aware of how other people experience the world. I wouldn't have had to pay attention to any of that, but because I am transgender, I did.

Yet there was also a scenario in which even as a transgender man I could have fallen into notions of masculinity and manhood that weren't healthy. Had I been born (or transitioned) a few years later, I would have had access to different conversations about masculinity, different online sources, and different perspectives. Had I been transitioning in a less diverse area, had I been more isolated from other trans people, had I learned about masculinity solely from online conversations, there is a world in which I, too, might have been taken in by thinkers who uphold the supremacy of men and their difference from women.

Instead, I came of age and transitioned as part of a lesbian community (which had its own challenges), on a burgeoning internet, and in a city where there was a diverse transmasculine community. These experiences helped me to more fully understand the masculinity I was transitioning into and avoid some of the pitfalls I could have easily stepped into had I not had the support and challenges of some of my community.

Even with all of that support, I struggled. I often felt invisible and left out of conversations. I felt that masculinity wasn't something it was okay to want. Even before the upswing of people using the term *toxic masculinity*, it felt like that's how many people viewed men—as toxic and the problem. So what did it mean that I felt like I was one of them?

I didn't have a lot of models in my personal life of what it could look like to be a man. My father died when I was very young, my stepfather hadn't treated my mother well and then bailed on our family, and my grandfather (probably the best example of masculinity in my life) faced his own pressures living up to what his culture and church taught about being a man, and by the time I began my transition he had passed away as well. I didn't have anyone I could talk to about what it meant to be a man. I tried to absorb as much as I could from the culture around me—movements, books, popular media (much of which I'll talk about in this book)—but so many of the models I was presented with just didn't feel right. They felt like not enough or like they were leaving things out.

As the conversation about masculinity has continued over the years, it seems to have only gotten more complicated. The rising numbers of books about gender, in general, and masculinity, in particular, often frame things in absolutes. As I read books about gender written by cisgender writers (of various genders), there are so many assumptions made about gender, so many things taken as unchangeable without examining where those ideas came from. Writers are often split into camps of biology or cultural convention without drawing out the intense interplay between those two camps. Even progressive books, ones aimed at helping us have conversations about equality in our households or freeing ourselves from constraints of gender roles, still seem to assume some kind of primal wiring that makes men and women drastically different from one another. It's as if we've lost the ability to speak with nuance about gender. This inability to deal with nuance isn't new, even if it does feel accelerated and amplified by social media and online discourse. Grappling with my own identity in the midst of these competing forces felt fraught. I was coming of age in a time when our language about gender identity was just entering the mainstream. As a transgender person, I often feel as if people are projecting onto me their own notions, experiences, and struggles with gender. Many times, these projections have nothing to do with my actual lived experience or behavior. I am simply a stand-in for the things people have been taught or felt. It seems many men are experiencing something similar as the online discourse about masculinity spills over into our daily lives, and we wonder if anyone actually sees us in the midst of the discourse. Is there a space for us to struggle? To have questions? To fail?

These complicated narratives about gender can have real-world consequences. I remember, vividly, the first time I saw a transmasculine person represented on screen.

When I was in my early twenties, I watched the film *Boys Don't Cry*. Based on the true story of Brandon Teena, a young person thought to be a transgender man, the film stars Hilary Swank as Brandon. *Boys Don't Cry* was the first film to highlight anything about transmasculine life (even though the film never uses the word *trans*), and it became a touchpoint for both the trans community and the general public. But that touchpoint is fraught.

The story of the film is complicated. The film, written and directed by Kimberly Peirce, is based on an article in the *Village Voice* about Brandon's murder. The article, written by Donna Minkowitz, has a complicated legacy. In the article, Minkowitz incorrectly portrayed Brandon not as a trans man, but as a lesbian who disliked her body due to childhood abuse. Minkowitz has now apologized for how she wrote that article. She says:

> Why did I assume this, besides transphobic ignorance? In brief, I was projecting. Reader, I was sexually abused as a child, and I at certain points in my life have identified with stone butches because the intensity of genital sensations was too painfully overwhelming for me to want or be able to continue to experience genital touching. For a chunk of my life, I was greatly frustrated, I was resentful about what I experienced as diminished pleasure, and I projected this frustration and resentment onto Brandon. Obviously, I also projected my own experience of sexual abuse on to his, and used it to concoct my own biased theory of trans origins.

Both Minkowitz and Peirce saw in the story of Brandon some of their own story of gender nonconformity, of lesbian identity, and that identification shaped how the film was made.

Several transgender men auditioned for the role of Brandon, but Peirce rejected all of them in favor of Hilary Swank, a cisgender woman. In a 2019 interview, she says, "I auditioned drag kings, I auditioned trans people, everybody. At the time, it was insane that my vision of the movie was that I would cast a trans person. But I just thought, I'm going to find somebody who lives the way Brandon does. Whatever we have to do to get there, we will. When I finally made the choice of the person that I chose, it was only because that person came the closest to bringing to life the person that we all wanted to bring to life." It's telling to me that the cisgender director believed a cisgender actor could better embody Brandon than the trans men who auditioned. It speaks to how our notions of gender and trans identity are shaped by the assumptions we bring to the process.

Hilary Swank was respectful of Brandon and used the correct pronouns for him throughout the press for the film. In her Oscars acceptance speech, she said, "I want to thank Brandon Teena for being such an inspiration to us all. His legacy lives on through our movie to remind us to always be ourselves, to follow our hearts, to not conform. I pray for the day when we not only accept our differences, but we actually celebrate our diversity. Thank you very much." At the same time, because Swank was nominated and won in the category of Best Actress, those less aware of the trans community were led to believe that Brandon, too, was simply playacting at being a boy.

When I watched this film, I was unaware of any of the conversations around it, but I knew how it made me feel. I was a student at a conservative Christian college. I was becoming more and more aware that something was different about me. I knew I was mostly attracted to women, and I felt more comfortable dressing in masculine clothing. I also knew that no one else seemed to feel like I did—until I saw Brandon on that screen. I heard him articulate his discomfort with his body, how he felt more comfortable in his masculine clothing and identity, how he loved women. For just a moment, I realized maybe there were other people in the world like me.

As the film progressed, I watched as the people in the town turned on him, outing him, sexually assaulting him, and then, finally, murdering him. I remember lying on my couch, unable to move, and thinking, *That's what happens to people like me. I might not be alone, but if I am myself, it will get me killed.*

I still believe that seeing *Boys Don't Cry* when and where I did kept me from coming out earlier. I tried to ignore my growing discomfort with my body. I told myself I could just be a genderqueer woman, and I didn't need to think more deeply about my gender than that. It worked, for a while.

I came out as a lesbian and entered into the queer community. Spending more and more time in women-only spaces made me realize how unlike other women I felt. I didn't feel connected to my femininity. I didn't feel connected to my body. I loved women, but I didn't love myself as a woman. But what did *that* mean? Could you love women, be a feminist, and still reject your own femininity? If I transitioned, didn't that mean turning my back on all of these people I claimed to love and support? Didn't that mean I was saying something terrible about women?

When I was beginning to consider the fact that I was transgender, I wrote a list of questions in my journal. Some of them were: "Do I really want this? Am I actually trans? Would passing as male make me more complete? What will T do to my body? Is there any way to predict what the T will do? Will T be enough? How do I feel about being male? How is one male? What makes someone male? Will T change my personality? Will T change me emotionally? Will I just be cashing in for heterosexual privilege?" These questions made me anxious. They filled me with doubt and fear. I didn't know who I could talk to about them. The people in my life, even the ones from the queer community, didn't really seem to understand.

I was terrified to transition. Some of those reasons were personal: fear of my family's reaction, of not being allowed to see my young siblings, and of how it would affect my career in the church. But beyond those personal fears hung a larger dread that hummed with the pressures of culture.

I had come out in the midst of leaving the conservative Christianity of my youth and young adulthood and didn't have many friends outside of that world. When I met Amy, the cousin of a friend of mine and the woman who would become my first wife, she became my window and entry into queer community. Almost all of her friends were women. There seemed to be, in this community, a low-level distrust of and distaste for men. It went beyond preference for the company of (and relationships with) women to a judgment of masculinity. I didn't fully understand it at the time, but as I became aware of my own identity, I felt implicated in it.

I began to read as many books by trans men as I could. One of the first was *The Testosterone Files: My Hormonal and Social Transformation from Female to Male* by Max Wolf Valerio. The book is split into two main parts: "Before Testosterone" and "After Testosterone." Short chapters bounce from topic to topic as Valerio shares anecdotes from his transition. Some of what I read in the "After Testosterone" section alarmed me.

In one chapter, he writes about seeing a woman and being overtaken by lust. He writes, "No wonder guys lose it sometimes, I think. How can they not? In the beginning, I think this a lot. My god, if this is how men feel, how come they don't rape more often? Rape and plunder. Take." He immediately goes on to say, "It is wrong to rape. I knew that before; I know that still. Any man who acts out these fantasies or impulses, no matter how strong, is doing a wrong act, an abominable act, and should be punished. Even so, I understand now the force of will it can take to keep from running wild with these feelings, the temptation." Reading that made me feel sick to my stomach. No matter how much he protested that he knew rape was wrong, this sense that he somehow understood the compulsion because of his experience on testosterone chilled me. Was this what my life would become? Was this who I would become?

It didn't help that this way of thinking matched some of the things I had heard from men growing up in my church. They were fond of saying that it was only their faith in Jesus that kept them from being rapists and murderers. These statements were meant to show how strong their faith was, but it also made me wonder about their underlying character. Was it really just Jesus that was holding these urges at bay? Did testosterone have the ability to turn a person into a monster?

On the other side were the strained conversations happening in the lesbian community. When I transitioned around 2008, there wasn't a lot of public awareness of trans men. Most people's only touchpoint was still *Boys Don't Cry*.

While the rise of the trans-exclusionary radical feminists (TERFs) was still in the early stages, their ideology was subtly present even in folks who would later affirm trans identities. There was an anxiety about butch women feeling the pressure to conform to masculinity and transitioning. Underneath that anxiety was something larger about gender, identity, and community—complex conversations about visibility, privilege, and who belonged where. It seemed some people believed that trans men transitioned because it was easier than being seen as gender nonconforming. They were abandoning women and the lesbian community to become part of the "traitor class." They were everything that was wrong with the world.

This rhetoric, even said jokingly, couldn't help but take a toll on me. It seemed as if transitioning would exclude me from all communities. I wondered where I would belong. If the church no longer wanted me, and the queer community rejected me, and the straight community thought I was weird or worthy of violence, then where would I find my people?

I remember sitting in a session at the Philadelphia Transgender Wellness Conference about prosthetics for transgender men; devices we could wear to feel more confident and comfortable. In a discussion group, someone who said their identity was genderqueer dominated the discussion and talked about how disgusting penises were. I shrunk back in my seat, feeling like I was in a place where I was supposed to be safe to discuss, to want, to share, yet I was being not only talked over but also told my desires were disgusting. I wondered if there was a place for me in my own community, if there was ever going to be a space where I could bring all of myself without having to wonder if I was going to be judged.

There were other situations, too, where I felt I couldn't talk about the unique pressures I was facing. If I spoke with non-trans folks about how I was having hot flashes or my face was breaking out or I was embarrassed to speak in class because my voice was cracking, I got jokes about how puberty was hard for everyone.

If I shared deeper concerns about getting misgendered a lot or worrying about how my family was going to react, I worried they would think I was regretting my transition. I had to keep up a positive face so no one would think I was second-guessing myself.

At the same time, there were other pressures I didn't know how to talk about. Everyone assumed I had white male privilege now. People assumed I was no longer afraid to walk home alone at night or that I blended in and no longer had to worry about being harassed for my queerness. It was assumed that whatever I was struggling with paled in comparison to every other group on the planet and so I should just be quiet.

I went from being considered a woman in very conservative spaces (where I was also told to just be quiet) to being considered a white man who shouldn't have any problems (so I should be quiet). Where was the space for me to struggle? To find community? To feel seen?

I felt invisible, often even in my own community, and because of that, there were also moments when, because I didn't feel my struggles were being taken seriously, I was resistant to or unable to hear valuable critique that would have allowed me to be kinder or a better partner to the people around me. I was so stuck in my own angst that I blamed other people for not getting it, unable to acknowledge that they, too, had experiences of oppression and alienation. They, too, felt unheard and unlistened to.

This is where I think my experience and that of cisgender men overlap and where my story begins to illuminate the experience of cisgender men. I, too, have felt the pain of feeling like my struggles didn't matter. I have wondered where I fit in a world that seems to change more rapidly than I can wrap my head around. I have wondered what it means to be a *good man* when it seems like people consider that those two words are unable to go together.

As I have struggled and grown and searched for a place for myself, as I've looked at all sorts of models to tell me who and what I can be, as I've tried to be good, what I've learned most intensely and vitally is that I cannot do this alone.

So often we frame masculinity and being a good man as something done in isolation. It's something we work on by ourselves. It's something we grow into. It's something we find through discipline. And if we're not getting it right, it's a personal failing.

The reality is both simpler and more complex than that; masculinity is built in community. The struggles that face us as men are both individual and societal. We can work on ourselves (and often need to), but we cannot do it all alone. As we work on ourselves, we also need to work on our culture. A culture of silence, a culture of alienation, a culture of anger and entitlement, a culture of learned incompetence. At every step, we do what we can to change while also changing the culture around us so we can all move more freely.

As I think about what I've learned about what it means to be a good man, it's both communal and my own intention. This combination, community and self-growth, is the key to a future of healthy masculinity.

For a long time I wanted someone to come and tell me what to do: how to be a good man, how to feel okay in my masculinity, how to be myself and also honor people of other genders. I wanted someone to come and save me from my bumbling, from my confusion, from my angst about my identity in a world that seemed to keep changing faster than I could get a handle on it. Then I realized that I had to save myself. I had to approach my gender with intention, figuring out what kind of man I *wanted* to be, figuring out how to be a *good man*. I had to put in the work. No one else could do it for me. The good news is I didn't have to do it alone. I could tap into a community of other men, including other trans men, so we could figure out how to work on ourselves while being in relationships with people who could help hold us accountable to the values we said we wanted to espouse.

Men need to have spaces where we can talk openly, honestly, and freely about the issues we face and the struggles we have. We need those spaces to be about us, though, and not about how everyone else sucks and is the reason we're oppressed. Our communal conversations need to focus on what we need to change, how we can be better, and how we can continue to adapt to a changing world and changing conceptions and perceptions of masculinity.

It's often said that as men go, so goes the world. That demonstrates why this is important work—it means that men still have outsized power and control over the world (while being half of the population). It also means that as men struggle and fall behind (which we're currently doing at rapid rates), we're at risk of taking everyone else down with us.

We have a responsibility to step up and to take a hard look at ourselves. We need to put in the work to be better men, better partners (not just romantically but in our friendships and working relationships as well), and better humans, not just for our own sakes but also for the sake of everyone around us. Because of our historic power and privilege (even when that power and privilege are sometimes tempered by race and class, men still hold them over women), we continue to send ripple effects through all of our relationships.

While my stories about masculinity are unique to my experience of being a transgender man in the world, I share them because I think they highlight the tension of talking about masculinity and gender. We all have our own stories of the things we've heard and been taught about our identities. The world is full of messages about what it means to be a man. We are buffeted on all sides about what masculinity means, what it should mean, and how we should live it out. We're surrounded by ideas and opinions about nature versus nurture, the role of chromosomes and hormones, and how much biology means (or doesn't mean).

We might feel like we have no choice, that everything is already laid out for us from our culture or our hormones or our biology or our family. It might feel like there is nothing we can do, that we are at the mercy of everything and everyone else to simply live out our identity. But here's what my experience has taught me: We can choose. We can choose what our masculinity means to us. We can choose how to live it out. We can choose to embody it in new ways. We can choose to be the kind of men we've only been able to dream of.

The gift of transitioning has been not only the gift of coming home to myself but also the gift of getting to be intentional about how I want to show up in the world. Since it felt like no one really wanted me to exist as a transgender man, I got to choose my own adventure. I've been able to really think through what my masculinity means to me and how I want to embody it. That experience of intentionality has shown me that the same is open to all of us. We can all think deeply about our identity and our bodies and how we live in this world. We can all make choices that allow us to be our best selves. We can all make changes to be more at home.

We are not at the mercy of our hormones or our churches or our families or our society. We are the makers of our lives. We get to intentionally choose. So let us choose well.

CHAPTER TWO

Naming the Wound

As I left college and came into adulthood, my world was women. I was learning more and more what it was like to move through lesbian spaces. On the one hand, this felt totally comfortable: as a queer/trans person (even without that language) growing up in fundamentalism, I was used to being in gendered spaces. And now that I was allowed to be in those spaces without having to hide or conceal my attraction to women, there was an element of freedom and ease. But at the same time, there was also a disconnect; there was something about these spaces that didn't feel right. I felt out of place. I felt like their connection with femininity wasn't something I shared. But that didn't make sense because I was, after all, fundamentally the same as them, right? Everyone expected me to be and feel the same as the rest of the women in these rooms, but no matter how hard I tried, I felt distance.

So once again, in the space I should have felt at home, I didn't. And I couldn't entirely explain why because none of it made sense. I was raised in this body. I was socially trained to be a woman. I was expected to be recognized as someone who should move through these spaces with comfort, and yet I didn't.

This feeling, this inexplicable lack of comfort, leads me to knowing that gender is something so much more complex than hormones, chromosomes, or brain science. I have a deep *knowing* of myself as a man that can't entirely be explained. I know I am a man.

I just want to be myself. And when I get super quiet—when I erase all of the messages telling me who I should be, who I can be, who I should want to be—when I get all of that out of my head and simply ask "how do I want to be seen?" every answer is "as a man." And it's actually more than that; it's not that I want to be *seen* as a man. It's just that I *am* one.

How, you might ask, do I know—especially since I never articulated that as a child and didn't latch on to it immediately once I knew transgender men existed? It's a fair question. A common talking point right now is that kids are being pressured into being trans. That as soon as they say one gender-nonconforming thing, people are asking them if they want hormones. That's just not true.

When I first started to think I might be transgender, what kept me from diving in sooner was all of the social pressure. It was the worry about how I would be treated by society; it was the worry of being ostracized from my family; it was the fear of not being accepted anywhere, not even in the LGB community. I saw the vitriol against transgender people around the Michigan Womyn's Music Festival; I saw how Max was talked about and treated in *The L Word*; I heard people say things like, "You've been in that body long enough; surely you can just continue." No one was encouraging me to be transgender. No one was pushing me into medical treatment. If anything, there was a hope that I would go to therapy and be told I wasn't trans.

As I wrote in chapter one, there was also a lot of pushback in my circles around the idea of masculinity. As I moved through the world and in my seminary classes, I was surrounded by guys, many of whom were trying to do it differently, but it seemed even they couldn't always articulate what they were trying to change.

At the same time, all of my closest friends were women. I was still part of the lesbian community. People still mistook me for a woman. There were lots of resources on feminism. There were academic texts and pop culture movements. There were the Riot Grrrls and the lesbian folk scene. There were scores of people talking about all the different types of ways to be a woman. There were resources for standing up to patriarchy, fighting back against the system, and taking care of each other. I read and learned so much from those sources, but they didn't speak to my experience of gender. At the same time, I didn't want to abandon those women's spaces. I didn't want to abandon or betray my friends. But I also knew I wasn't one of them. I had never been one of them, even when they assumed I was.

Among men, I didn't feel like I could talk about masculinity, not really, even as I was hungry to talk about it. It didn't feel like there was a space to unpack it in the same way there was in the lesbian and feminist communities I was now leaving—where masculinity was often discussed as a problem or a negative, but at least it was being discussed. It was like men were everywhere, dominating every conversation, but there was nothing of substance being said. We weren't unpacking what it was to be a man.

As I began my transition, I realized I could decide what type of man I wanted to be. I had a freedom to craft my masculinity from scratch. This was both a blessing and a curse: a blessing because I could be who I wanted and needed, a curse because the reason I could choose this is because no one saw me as a man. Actually, it was more than that—so many people didn't want me to be a man even though I was. I didn't have a community of men teaching me and saying, "This is what it's like to be one of us." I simply faced a wall of silence. Excluded from the inner circles. Shunned from the citadels of masculinity. Scolded by those who didn't think I belonged. Pushed back by those who wanted me to stay in my place.

And yet I think the idea I had that there was this mythical passing on of knowledge about what it means to be a man, that it's handed down from fathers to sons forever and ever amen, wasn't the truth either. I think many men do exactly what I did to construct their masculinity: They look around and try to copy what they see. They watch movies and read novels; they emulate the celebrities they admire; they watch their fathers and the other men in their lives and try to mimic them well enough to not call attention to themselves.

Certainly cisgender men were privy to conversations I wasn't, spaces I wasn't, and yet I'm not sure it helped. Listening to them talk, later, about what they had learned, I got the sense the things they saw confused them. They tried to play it off, but the way they moved led me to believe there was something broken not just in *what* they learned but in the *way* they had learned.

There were the horror stories, of course—fathers who tried to toughen up their sons, who were emotionally distant or even violent. But more than anything, it seemed there was a silence. We didn't talk about feelings. We didn't talk about what being a man meant to us. We didn't talk. And in that silence grew a sense of unease. Never sure they were doing it right. Never sure they were living up to the unnamed expectations. Always feeling like they weren't measuring up but not even sure what they were trying to measure up to.

In their stories, I heard my own: Am I man enough? What does that even mean? How will I know if I am doing it right? What if all the naysayers are right, and I'm not really a man? What then? Where will I go? What will I do? Will I ever feel like I'm enough?

This question—will I ever feel like I'm enough?—seems to be the one thing all men have in common. This deep-seated terror that they don't fit anywhere, that they don't live up to anything, that they are failing. Failing.

But failing at what, exactly? Being the very thing that is supposed to come the easiest. Being yourself.

As I looked around, I also knew that the type of masculinity I was often seeing on display wasn't right. A masculinity that spoke over women, considered them less than, saw them as objects for men's pleasure—that was not the type of masculinity I wanted to inhabit.

As I started my medical transition, I began to think deeply about what being a man meant to me. What kind of man was I going to be? What did being a man even mean? How could I learn what it meant to be a man without many models? I began to look more closely at the interactions I was having with the men in my life and paying attention to how they were changing.

A strange thing happened when I started my transition. At the time, I was married to a woman who had a close relationship with her family. We spent lots of holidays at their house. Her stepfather was what I would consider a "man's man." He was a bit rough and tumble. He was someone who worked with his hands. He was a volunteer firefighter and had been for years. He had always been nice to me, but our relationship wasn't particularly close. But when I started my transition, something changed. On the one hand, he would shake my hand instead of hugging me. The physical norms shifted. But on the other hand, he started to speak to me differently. I remember sitting with him in the audience at one of my partner's concerts. He started to tell me about some medical stuff he was going through, but it wasn't just about the procedures; it was also about how he was feeling. Another time I mentioned potentially being interested in firefighting, and he promised to do whatever he could to make a space for me and get me connected. It was like suddenly I made sense to him in a way I hadn't before, and in that making sense, some of his walls came down. I was someone in whom he could confide.

This has happened to me other times as well. The men in a family who drive everyone else a little nuts are extra kind to me. I understand the tension here. I understand the hypocrisy. I understand how fraught all of this is to name. At the same time, it is incredibly affirming of my identity. I feel seen by them in a way I often don't feel seen by women, even women who theoretically are more supportive of transgender people. They instead see me as somehow defective. Not really a man. A failed woman. I don't belong anywhere in their world, but with the men, I make sense.

It's complicated because I don't always fit in with the men either. I have a whole different experience of my life. I've been socialized differently. I value centering women. And yet I also value being seen. How do you make space for yourself when it feels like only one group of people really sees you? How do I make sense of the fact that my ex's stepfather wasn't always the kindest to the women in his life, but he was vulnerable and kind to me? What do I do with all of that?

There are no easy answers here, but I think paying attention to what's happening is instructive. So much goes unnoticed for cisgender people. So much goes unsaid. Transgender people have the ability to see and speak because we are paying attention. We see all of the things that happen under the surface. We see how people's attitudes toward us change depending on how we look or what they know about our history. We see how people move differently through different worlds and with different gendered groups almost without thinking. So we can also assess with more nuance the resources out there that are trying to help us understand our masculinity.

One of the first sources I turned to in my attempt to understand masculinity was *Iron John* by Robert Bly. This book was first released in 1990, but it feels like it comes from a much earlier time. Bly recounts the story of "Iron John," one of Grimm's fairy tales, about a young prince who forms a relationship with a wild man.

Bly is someone who was really trying to get it right. He wanted to be sensitive and in tune with what the feminist movement had changed while also paying attention to how men hadn't kept pace with those changes. He talks about how his book isn't just for straight, cisgender men, but, almost without exception, every example he uses is of a straight, cisgender man. The book as a whole is about men's relationships with women. There are passing mentions of men's relationships with one another, but they generally involve competing with each other for the love of a woman.

Bly takes the story of Iron John to be a larger myth about the stages of life that men go through. Bly, like others, creates a hero's journey for men, a way of mythologizing the journey to manhood. He also draws on a kind of vague, homogenized idea of "tribal cultures" and their initiation rites for boys.

What drew me to the book was its frank conversation about men, particularly the wounding of men. Bly spends a lot of time talking about the *wound*, the places where men have been injured, often by other men in their lives. He talks about the absence of father figures.

It makes sense to me why this book would have resonated at the time (though, in revisiting it in order to write this book, I realized I had never actually finished reading it the first time through). When I first encountered this book, I had read a bunch of memoirs by transgender men, and I was hungry for something different. I knew how some trans men were figuring out their masculinity, but I wanted to hear from cisgender men. It felt important to attune myself to their conversations as I figured out what I wanted my own masculinity to look like.

I resonated with the conversations about the absent father. My own father died by suicide when I was very young, and my stepfather was mostly aloof. He was trapped in his own immaturity and wounding and was never quite able to grow up. He ended up having an affair and leaving our family. Later on, he would blame me for his affair, saying that I (as a four-year-old) had never accepted him as my father, and that's why, twelve years later, he cheated. Yes, that logic doesn't really track for me either. What I saw was a man who was unable to take any responsibility for his own actions, who blamed all of his bad behavior on other people. If it wasn't my mother making him do it, it was me or maybe the devil.

Growing up in a high control religion, I was also primed to believe lots of things were caused by absent fathers: homosexuality, for one. I was made to feel I was deeply wounded because of my lack of a father.

After the divorce, every year on Father's Day, I received some kind of message about how God could be the perfect Father, and so therefore I didn't need a dad on earth. That maybe seemed well and good, but when all of the families did the father/child mini-golf outing, I was very aware of the fact that God wasn't standing next to me with a putter.

I also received conflicting messages about how, since I didn't have a good dad on earth, it would be harder for me to understand the love of God as a perfect Father. God could be both a substitute and someone hard to conceive of.

I deeply felt the wounding Bly talks about.

One of the issues with Bly's book is a sense that women (especially mothers) are to blame for a lot of what has gone wrong in men's lives. There is the overbearing mother the boy needs to separate himself from, then the women he chases after who aren't the "right" woman, and then finally there is the "Woman with the Golden Hair" who will somehow complete him. This narrative of women harming and then saving men is not the solution we need.

In Bly's story, our manhood seems to depend on our relationships with women—masculinity as the pursuit of women. We talk about women in terms of conquest and conquering, of having sex, of having power over, of having a woman in our thrall. This is why so many queer men are automatically counted as "less than" men because they have no interest in those types of relationships with women. In this way of thinking, our masculinity comes from having power over a whole group of people. It's not something internal; it's something we try to prove by how we respond to other people.

Basing our own sense of self on how other people react to us or the relationships we have with them is a recipe for disaster. We will continue to struggle and search and hope that someone else can bestow on us the feelings we feel we're lacking. We will continually wait for someone else to make us feel like the person we need to be. Maybe this is why many men are ready to fight at a moment's notice, why they swagger and talk a certain way around men they perceive as more powerful than they are: they are trying to win favor with someone who can grant them what they feel they are lacking. This behavior puts us out of alignment with ourselves and puts us into weird relationships with the men around us. We can't be in right relationship with them because we are always using them to prove something to ourselves and the people around us.

These types of striving are what many people have rightly called *toxic*. They rely on power, domination, and hierarchy. They rely on men being above people of other genders; they rely on white men being above men of other races; they require that we never question or challenge the systems as they currently are—the systems that, by the way, aren't actually serving any of us. It's these same systems of power and hierarchy that make it impossible for men to be vulnerable enough to admit they need to see a doctor, or talk to a therapist, or put less stress on themselves to lead or be strong or bold or brave.

It's these systems that make men feel they need to compete with one another instead of supporting one another. It's these systems that cause men to question whether or not they've beat out enough other people or subjugated enough women or had enough sex to actually consider themselves a man. But to question the systems would cause us to question everything, and that feels scary, so we contort ourselves to make it work. We try to prove ourselves over and over again. We try to be tougher, or we say we don't care what those other guys think anyway (even as we still feel like things aren't quite right in us).

Another question that seems to plague men is, *when* am I a man? How do we know when we've reached manhood? Is it when we leave our parents' house? Go off to college? Get our first job? Is it when we get married or have a long-term partner for the first time? Does "becoming a man" have to do with sex and sexuality? Or with other expressions of physical prowess?

Robert Bly's solution to these questions in *Iron John* is to say men need initiation rituals. He tells stories from "tribal cultures" about how they initiate their boys into manhood.

The problem with Bly's push for rites of passage is twofold. The first is the kind of vague cultural appropriation Bly practices. He never shares exactly what culture he's taking this initiation rite idea from, how these rites play into larger cultural understandings, and if those rites are open to other cultures. This vague sense that other cultures have it figured out and we just need to take from them is pure white supremacy. For white people, we won't get free by continuing our history of stealing things that don't belong to us.

The other problem with Bly's talk of initiation rites is they seem to be rooted in male violence, in the separation of men and women (and a shoring up of differences and distinctions), and in causing injury to children so they can take on adult roles. He tells stories of young boys being starved, left in the woods alone, shunned by their mothers, and then injured by the men of the community.

In some ways, it feels similar to the way the military talks about boot camp or West Point talks about initiation of its new students: you break down the individual so you can mold them into the way you want them to be. This usually involves some kind of physical hazing, pushing people to their physical limits and trying to see if they will break mentally.

Pushing ourselves physically can sometimes have benefits—training for a marathon or an elite athletic competition. It shows us the meaning of commitment, that we're often capable of more than we ever believed and that we can persevere. The best training, though, also teaches us to listen to our bodies, to know when to push and to know when to stop pushing because it will cause injury. In these hazing rites, saying no is akin to failure.

Are we only men if we have suffered physically? Are we only men if we've managed to prove ourselves to other men who are bigger, stronger, or have more power than us? I don't think so.

One thing that Bly's book gets right is that men do need to deal with their wound—though I'd also argue there are some problems in the way he talks about this idea.

In *Iron John*, Bly wants us to externalize the wound—to turn it into a coming-of-age ritual, to make it physical, to be able to point to an actual scar. His reasoning, I think, is that if the wound is externalized, it makes it easier to deal with. We can point to the scar and say, "See? This thing happened to me, and I survived it!" And then men will rally around us and say, "Yes, we see it! You're one of us now. You're enough. You're a man." But in this way, Bly normalizes the brutality that he seems, in other places, to want to question. He anchors maleness in violence and harm. Men become men, in his estimation, by going through some terrible physical ordeal, by being shunned by their mothers, and by being mistreated by the older men in their community. Once they survive the trauma, they are ready to take roles of leadership because they have undergone the trial.

Almost all men do, indeed, have a wound. In large ways and small ways, the world has been brutal to us. Some of us suffered abuse at the hands of people who were supposed to love and protect us. Some of us were born into a world that doesn't see our goodness because of our race or sexuality or gender expression. Some of us were brutalized by systems (poverty, systemic racism, foster care, police brutality). Some of us were brutalized by other boys and men and told to "man up" to stop being a [insert feminine-gendered slur of your choice here], to stop crying, to toughen up. Some of us were bullied emotionally, and others were bullied physically.

We have wounds from society, from the men in our lives, from our own growing pains. We carry them inside us, tucking them out of sight. Many of us try to pretend they don't exist. We don't talk about them or acknowledge them, and because of that, we form our lives around them. Our refusal to acknowledge them causes the wound to fester and grow.

Often, we take our wound out on others. We lash out. We hide ourselves away. We tell the next generation to "man up," to be strong, to stop their crying. We repeat the cycle so that other men hurt like we hurt.

Bly is right that we need to acknowledge our wounds. We need to tend to them. We need to work on healing them, not just alone but in community as well. But this isn't about stealing a "coming of age" ceremony from a culture we don't belong to or externalizing the wound by walking on hot coals or fasting—this is about doing the hard emotional work of healing from trauma. We acknowledge the harm that's been done to us, we pay attention to how it has shaped (and continues to shape) how we show up in the world, and we break the cycles so we don't pass on this wounding to another generation of men.

We must acknowledge our wounds. Identify them, name them, sit with them, make space for them. Instead of pushing them down or trying to overcome them with strength, we allow our wounds to be seen, first by ourselves and then by others. We recognize how we've been shaped by our wounds and how we've changed our shape to compensate for those wounds. We pay attention to the ways these coping mechanisms are no longer serving us.

Then we share our wounding with people we trust. We open up conversations about how we've been hurt and how we've tried to manage that hurt. By starting to bring these wounds to the light we begin, ever so slowly, to heal them.

The real hero's journey isn't about going on a grand adventure, battling monsters, and facing trials. It's about being willing to go on a deep inner journey. It's about battling the demons in our own lives and being willing to do the hard work of healing. It's about facing up to the places where we are perpetuating harm. Then it's about working to repair the harm, not only for ourselves but also for the good of the community.

The idea of the hero's journey ends with the hero returning home. He returns home changed by his experiences and bearing a gift for his community. If men are to take seriously the work that is ours to do, it will require allowing ourselves to be changed, doing the work of healing. Only then will we be able to be agents of goodness, healing, and wholeness to the people and communities we love. If we skip any part of the journey, if we refuse to examine our wounding, if we refuse to admit that we sometimes cause harm and perpetuate cycles of harm, then we will be unable to provide the necessary gift to our people.

But if we are willing, then we can start to really change things. We'll no longer be at the mercy of our wounds and the people and systems who gave them to us. We'll be able to be free and, in our freedom, help others find their own way.

CHAPTER THREE

Finding Safety in Our Bodies

In early transition, I desperately wanted to be seen as the man that I was, but I was constantly worried people didn't see me that way. I started my transition in graduate school, and while the people closest to me were completely unsurprised when I came out, the wider community didn't know me or see me in the same way.

Even though I was relatively new to understanding myself as a man, now that I had the language, it made the rest of my life make sense. I was struck with this overwhelming sense of wasted time. I felt like I'd been living my entire life in stasis, suspended in the goo of not knowing, and now that I knew, I was ready to live. I was ready to be seen as all of who I am. I didn't want to waste another second feeling invisible or being misgendered.

Now that I was able to name myself, it was hard for me to understand that I didn't necessarily look any different to the people around me. I finally made sense to myself, but this actually complicated me to other people. They looked at me and saw me as the person they'd known me as, but I didn't feel like that person anymore.

This disconnect in the way I was perceived led to pain as people struggled to use my new pronouns. (I didn't change my name, so they didn't have to change that.) I started to think constantly about how I was perceived. I braced myself any time someone was about to use a pronoun for me, whether in class or in social settings. As my transition progressed, the murky middle ground got harder and harder to take. I constantly wondered: How will people see me in this setting? Will I be gendered correctly? Even worse, will some people gender me correctly and others not, leading to a moment when I'll have to either out myself or let the confusion grow?

I became more and more anxious in social settings. Always an introvert, I became even less interested in going out. I went to class and then came home. I told people I didn't want to hang out. I refused to go to places where there would be a lot of people I didn't know.

When I did have to go out and be around people, I thought a lot about how I was being perceived. I started to pay attention to the things that got me gendered correctly. I realized if I talked and smiled a lot, I was more likely to be misgendered, so I taught myself to speak in a monotone voice; utter simple, short sentences; and smile less. I made less eye contact. I paid attention to how I walked, and I tried to take longer strides. I tried to take up more space (even as I worried about being like the other guys who take up too much space). I pitched my voice lower.

None of this was an act. I wasn't trying to put on masculinity; instead, I was trying to learn how to inhabit it. I was trying to make myself intelligible to others as I was finally intelligible to myself. I found that my physicality mattered in helping other people see me.

At the same time, this hypervigilance was exhausting. I worried that an errant gesture, a single upspeak in my sentences, a too open smile would give me away. And it wasn't just about being misgendered. There was also a very real fear for my physical safety. Being outed as transgender could put me in danger. I both wanted to be seen as who I am and wanted to get home safely. These two desires made me feel like hyperawareness was the only way to survive. I knew intimately the dance of watching how I show up, of examining every single one of my physical movements, of having a running ticker tape in my head of what I was doing at any given time. It's like standing outside of myself watching to make sure that I don't slip up.

I learned that the less I said, the better I was perceived as male. On the one hand, this pained me; I wanted to be as friendly as possible to every retail, restaurant, and bookstore worker I came across because I'd had those jobs, and I knew how much they can suck. But early in my transition, before the testosterone had deepened my voice, when I went into stores as I normally did, when I spoke as I'd been used to, I almost always got called *she* or *ma'am*, and I hated it. So I learned to answer in one-word sentences. I kept my voice as low as I could. I smiled, but my smile was more muted. Those behaviors got me coded as male, which was correct, and so I kept doing them.

But it did make me think about how much more restricted I am. Restricted from being friendly, restricted from conversation, restricted from smiling. I felt like I had less access to emotional range. It was a tradeoff but one I was willing to make in order to be seen as who I am. I wondered, though, about how much I was giving up and why certain things were assumed to be feminine. Why does my smile have a gender? Why does a fuller vocal range mean I'm feminine?

* * *

I don't think I'm the only guy who has made myself smaller to fit into a male box. Whether that's limiting your vocal range or limiting your emotional range or limiting the things you're interested in, many of us have felt we've had to shrink so as not to be excluded. Maybe it's giving up something you loved: a certain toy, participating in dance, even the "wrong" kind of sport. Maybe it's the way you tuck your emotions inside and don't talk about them, pushing down the things that are bothering you or causing you distress because you don't want to be seen as weak. Maybe it's not crying or laughing, even when you want to because you want to appear strong. Whatever it is that you're doing, it's shrinking yourself down to fit into a stereotype of masculinity. We like to say that all sorts of ways of being a man are acceptable, but in practice, we shrink ourselves down almost without thinking about it.

We do it because we're worried about what other men will think of us. How they'll treat us. If they'll consider us "enough" to call ourselves a man. Even as the very men we're worried about are worrying about the same things. This isn't good for us, restricting ourselves in this way. We don't have to live like this, making ourselves smaller in an attempt to win people over.

We do it thinking it makes us bigger and tougher when really it makes us weaker. What would happen if we stopped the mental math around "man enough" and instead just showed up? What if we showed up with all of our feelings? All of our interests? All of our embodied ways of being? What if we didn't worry about looking too feminine or gay or whatever else we say in order to make ourselves feel bad about a range of expression?

* * *

The place that taught me most about what range of expressions were allowed for men was the bathroom. Bathrooms became a minefield. In some respects, they had always been a minefield, but now it seemed they were more dangerous than ever. At this particular moment in time, I knew myself to be a man, but I hadn't yet started my medical transition, so I felt like I still needed to use the women's restroom. I figured if I did that, I probably wouldn't get assaulted, and if anyone really pushed, I would be able to show them my legal ID, which at that point still had an F on it.

When I was out with friends, I would often ask them to go into the bathroom with me. It felt like if we entered the bathroom talking to one another, it would be clear to anyone watching that I belonged in there. It's a safeguard that felt necessary.

I remember one moment so clearly. My partner at the time was singing in a women's choir, and I was traveling with them to support her at their concert. On the way home, we stopped at a restaurant for lunch, and I was very aware of the makeup of our group. I was aware of how I was being seen and gendered by strangers, and I was hit with a wave of anxiety about using the restroom. I asked my partner to go with me, and she rolled her eyes. She thought I was being silly, overreacting. I tried to explain the fear I felt, but she couldn't enter into it with me. She finally agreed to go with me, and I went as fast as I could, relieved that I'd made it through another public bathroom.

Later, once I was on testosterone but not always being seen as male consistently, bathrooms became the worst part of my day. I was never sure which one to use. I was never sure which one would be safest. When I started to use the men's room more often, suddenly I was thrust into an entirely new world. Gone were the clean floors and the fully stocked toilet paper. Gone were the sweet smells and the conversations of women. Men's restrooms were different. My sneakers stuck to the floor. I was afraid to touch anything, not knowing what might be crawling on the surface. Toilet seats were often wet and stained. I've learned to check and make sure there is toilet paper before I sit down.

But it's not just the cleanliness; it's the rules. There are rules in the men's room. You don't make eye contact. You don't say hello or smile. You do not talk. There are rules, too, about which urinals to use. You never stand next to each other; you always leave a buffer urinal. Even though I don't use the urinals, I've learned to pay attention to which stall I am using, and if there is someone in one, I leave a buffer.

I learned how to look at the floor. I learned to walk in as quickly as possible and walk out. I learned to blow my nose so that no one questions why a guy who's not pooping is pulling toilet tissue. I pay attention to how my pee sounds and worry that something in what I'm doing will out me as trans and put me at risk.

If a stall isn't available, I learned to wait with my eyes on the floor, praying that one will open quickly. I leave if there's too long of a wait.

Even now, fifteen years into my transition, there are bathrooms that strike fear in me. Bathrooms with doors that don't lock or stalls with no doors at all. Ones where there are huge gaps between the door and the stall wall. Any bathroom where it feels like there is no privacy.

It feels like of all the things that should strike fear in a person's heart, fulfilling basic biological needs should be at the bottom of the list. Shouldn't every person be able to walk into a clean, well-stocked restroom and have their choice between a stall and a urinal? Shouldn't every person be able to easily do their business with privacy and with the materials they need, then wash their hands (for the love of God, men, *wash your hands*) before going about their day? How did bathrooms become battlefields?

Transgender people know intimately the battlefield, but it's not just us. Cisgender men, too, internalize all sorts of rules around how to use the restroom safely. The codes around urinal use, no talking, no eye contact, and more make what should be a totally normal and stress-free experience into one that feels dangerous.

And isn't that the complicated thing? These gendered rules and spaces we've made into battlegrounds that absolutely don't have to be. There is no reason restrooms need to be weird. On one of my first trips to the Philadelphia Transgender Wellness Conference, I experienced the joy of all-gender restrooms. Certainly they were strange at first; you'd walk in and not know quite what to expect: Stall or urinals? Who would be in there? But once your initial shock subsided, there was a sense of ease. No one was watching you. No one was looking to see if you were out of place. No one was making judgments about whether or not you were using a stall or a urinal. There was no stress about making eye contact or how your pee sounded hitting the bowl or if anyone would tell you that you were in the wrong place.

Before you get nervous and say, "Well, what about people being assaulted in the restrooms?" Having more people of all genders in a space should serve to reduce risk. There are more people watching out for one another, more people simply doing their business. And let's be real, a sign on a door has never stopped anyone who is determined to assault someone. If you really want to hurt someone or break the law, you're not going to be dissuaded by a gendered space. But ungendering spaces makes it easier for a whole lot of people: the butch woman with the short hair, the mom with the adult son with disabilities, the father with his daughter, the married couple where one needs some help transferring from a wheelchair; all of these people can be served by all-gender restrooms.

While the early stages of transition are not an experience all men have, I thought I was the only one doing this, the only one hyperaware. Or at least that it wasn't something cisgender men do. They just show up, right? They take up space, they spread their legs, they don't think twice about their bodies. And for some men, this seems to be true, but many, many other men comment on feeling inhibited. Of being aware of their hands and bodies. (One might think this is only for "effeminate men," but the reality is so many people are worried about being policed for their movements and considered "effeminate" that it affects quite a lot of men.)

Here's the thing: when I transitioned, I didn't always know what the rules were in men's spaces. I had to relearn how to hold my body because I had internalized the patterns of women's spaces as a way to (attempt to) blend in and keep myself safe. But this process of relearning how to hold my body in men's spaces wasn't something that felt inauthentic or like trying to learn a way of being that didn't come naturally. Instead, it was about returning to how my body naturally moved. It was about coming back home to how I had wanted to be in my body all of those years. It was the way I felt more like myself when I wasn't trying to put on femininity. I was learning how to let myself take up space instead of shrinking myself down. Even as I was aware of how I was moving, I felt like I was allowed to be bigger.

Just a note for those folks who will say this was because I was trying to mimic femininity and play into a feminine stereotype instead of just allowing myself to be and that was why I was uncomfortable: it was about more than that. It wasn't that hyperfemininity wasn't the right fit but that some other kind of femininity was. Trust me, I tried to be butch. I tried to just be myself. But there was always something that felt off. Partly it was my body, but partly it was feeling like I was always having to leave some part of myself behind in order to be in women's spaces and be seen as a woman. I understand there are *lots* of ways to be a woman; I am just not one.

I believe we all have a way to be in our bodies that feels good and right to us. If we get quiet, if we allow ourselves to be comfortable, we find it. But so many of us are trying to mimic the bodies of those around us. For men, this often looks like making ourselves harder. Holding ourselves apart. Being tougher and stronger. We pretend to care more about sports so we have something to talk about on guys' night. We keep our emotions hidden away and don't talk about the things we're afraid of. Of course that plays out in our bodies as well: the playful punch to a buddy's shoulder, the way we pat someone on the back three times when we hug them (if we hug them), the playful wrestling we engage in. It's not that these things are always inauthentic, but they are just a sliver of the range of physicality we could engage in if we would let ourselves.

*　*　*

Even as some men take up more physical space, even as they don't think about where they have their arms or how much room they're taking up, even as they don't think about how they're entering a room, there is also a sense that men long for more ease in our bodies. It might seem like a bit of a contradiction because men are, generally, allowed to take up more space, to be freer in their skin, and to carry themselves however they please. But underneath that, for many of us, is a deep fear that we're somehow carrying our bodies wrong. From policing our gestures so we don't appear effeminate, to restraining ourselves from reaching out a hand or a hug to a friend, to worrying about how much affection we're allowed to share with our children or how much (and what kind) of emotion we're allowed to display; for all our *freedom*, we don't have a lot of *ease*.

We need to unlearn our fear of inadequacy. Our fear that we are somehow "not masculine enough" because of how we walk, talk, dress, or hold our bodies. Our fear that we aren't measuring up causes us to both hold ourselves apart from the people we long to be close to and sometimes overcompensate in unhealthy ways in order to prove to other people that we're enough. This cocktail leads us to both isolation and often toxic behavior as well.

For many of us, there is a deep-seated sense that we're not showing up in our bodies correctly. That other men are watching us and judging us and finding us wanting. We confine ourselves to smaller boxes, limiting what we allow to be acceptable expressions. Sometimes we show up with more aggression than we intend so no one thinks we're the weakest. Or we catch ourselves in a moment of freedom and pull back before anyone notices.

What if you could just be? What if there were no one judging you? Or, since we can't control other people, what if we stopped caring about being judged? What if we let any comments about our gestures just roll off of us? Easier said than done, I know. But it's vital that we both learn to allow ourselves more freedom and also change the culture of policing other people's physicality.

* * *

What are the limits of masculinity? When we talk about what "isn't manly," what are we talking about? Is it a way of being? A way of dressing? Is it like that senator who, when asked to define pornography, said, "I can't define it, but I know it when I see it"? If that's the case, whose seeing gets to define it for the rest of us?

Why is it that something that was perfectly acceptable as an expression of masculinity in one generation is completely unacceptable for a new generation? Who decides? Who enforces these rules, and how?

These questions might feel too esoteric or like I'm trying to play a "gotcha game," but they are actually designed to get us talking. For too long, there has been an assumption that we're all on the same page when it comes to gender. Everyone knows what it means to be manly, and even more importantly, everyone knows what it means to be unmanly. And even when we poke at that a little bit more, knowing that conceptions of acceptable gender behavior differ depending on your cultural context, on where you live, on your age, we still seem incapable (at best) or unwilling (at worst) to actually broach these questions honestly.

What are we afraid of, especially if so many of us are also living with a secret dread that we are falling outside of the bounds of "acceptable" masculinity? What will it cost us to consider these questions and see if we want to rethink our notions all together?

My experience as a trans man has helped me have more security in my masculinity because I've had to fight for it. My identity has been continually questioned: People call me names all the time. They question my masculine identity, they make fun of my name and my mannerisms, they've called me ugly and sick, they pretty consistently call me a woman. It's not pleasant, but it also doesn't shake my sense of self anymore. I know who I am, and I know that no one can take my identity away from me, not with name-calling or by refusing to acknowledge me. But it took a while to get to this place of confidence. In the beginning of my transition, I would have taken these insults as proof I wasn't doing masculinity right. I would have tried harder to be tougher, to speak lower, to even out my mannerisms. I would have been crushed by the comments calling my gender into question.

It took years, but now I move through the world knowing who I am. Because I am sure of my identity, I worry less about how I show up. I no longer try to pitch my voice down or speak in a monotone. I no longer worry that smiling at a store clerk will cause me to be misgendered. I don't care if people think I'm gay or that my mannerisms are "effeminate." I am simply myself, and because of that, I no longer hold myself apart from my friends. My relationships have gotten deeper, I'm more affectionate with the people in my life, and I feel more ease in my body. This happened because I first did the work to accept myself and to feel centered and enough in my own masculinity and the expression of it. Once I had done that, I was able to show up differently in public.

I think many of us are trapped in that fragile space of feeling like we need to prove ourselves. We have all of these voices in our heads: our fathers, our older brothers, the guys from the sports team at school, the bullies who made fun of anyone different, the people who said hurtful things about our bodies or our presentations. We worry, at all times, that we'll slip up, and it will call into question our masculinity.

Much of the fear we have around participating fully in life comes from people who try to create rigid structures that keep us in line. Think about the things you don't want to do or you're afraid to admit that you enjoy. How many of those are because you worry that other people will question your masculinity? Maybe you don't think about it in quite those terms, but you're worried about being called some kind of slur, you're worried someone will say that you're gay or soft or need to "man up." And if they do say those things to you, you feel self-conscious. You don't feel settled in your own sense of your gender, so you continually feel like you need to prove it to others.

*   *   *

This fear of being considered "less than" (or being considered too feminine) affects more than just how we carry our bodies and interact with the people around us. It's also affecting our job prospects and security. One of the fastest-growing sectors of work is health care. As the population continues to grow and people live longer lives, they will need more care as they age. Everything from nurses to home health-care aids to caregivers will be needed. It's a job with competitive wages where you can make a real difference in the lives of the people you're helping. And yet, because of the stigma that helping professions are "women's work," many men refuse to even consider these jobs. While many men drop out of the workforce or hope that certain industries will bounce back, other sectors are experiencing rapid and accelerating growth. It's not that jobs don't exist; it's that some men aren't even willing to consider the jobs that do exist.

In his book *Of Boys and Men*, Richard Reeves grapples with the complications of work and gender. He starts by saying, "Simply put, male jobs have been hit by a one-two punch, of automation and free trade. Machines pose a greater threat to working men than to women for two reasons . . . the occupations most susceptible to automation are just more likely to employ men."

But it's not just that those jobs are going away. Reeves goes on to say, "In 2020, STEM jobs accounted for 9% of U.S. employment among prime-age workers, while HEAL [health, education, administration, and literacy] jobs accounted for 23%. Health care and education are very large sectors, between them accounting for around 15% of all jobs . . . in terms of raw job creation, HEAL is outpacing STEM; by my calculations, for every new STEM job created by 2030 there will be more than three new HEAL jobs." He adds, "The number of nurses and nurse practitioners needed is expected to increase by about 400,000 by 2030." Not only that, but "in a survey conducted at the end of 2021 by the Chartis Center for Rural Health, 99% of rural hospitals reported staffing shortages, with 96% saying that recruiting and retaining nurses were their biggest challenges." In schools, too, we're seeing a rise of available jobs: "Two-thirds of school districts reported teacher shortages, in a survey of 1,200 school and district leaders conducted in 2021 by Frontline Education." As their fields are growing, the gender gap widens. Reeves states that "only 3% of pre-K and kindergarten teachers are men," and when it comes to nursing, the issue is "male nurses are also often stereotyped as effeminate or homosexual, or simply as failed doctors."

To refuse to provide for yourself and your family because the work seems "too feminine" is a problem. We can talk about unequal pay or lack of access to training that would make people qualified for many jobs, but in this situation, at least the biggest barrier to entry seems to be men's pride and egos and a fear of taking on work considered feminine.

It's only when we are secure in our own identity that we can explore more fully the world around us. Overcoming our fear of inadequacy will allow us to show up more in our relationships and walk away from behaviors that harm others.

* * *

Next time you are alone, spend some time paying attention to how you hold your body. What feels the most comfortable and natural? What feels uncomfortable or like you're trying something on? Are there ways you police your body when you're around your friends or out in public? Can you identify what you do and what you wish you could do? When you're alone, can you give yourself permission to do what feels right and natural?

Are there ways that you might want to try to hold your body if you didn't have to worry about anyone giving you grief over it? Maybe it's a way of crossing your legs or a gesture that used to feel right but that you've trained yourself out of. Maybe it's simply being more at ease or thinking less about what you're doing at every moment. Can you find some time and space to just let yourself be without worrying?

Once you've gotten more at ease while you're alone, are there a few people (or even one person) in your life you can let your guard down with? Someone who is also on a journey toward freedom or who supports you in your full expression?

Next time you're together, can you show up a little bit more fully? Turn off the voices in your head that tell you to watch yourself and instead just be. When those thoughts come up, remind yourself that you're safe and go back to being present.

What would change in your life if you never felt you had to prove yourself? If you didn't feel like you could fail in your masculinity? If, however you are a man, it's enough?

CHAPTER FOUR

Unlearning Learned Incompetence

One of the things I am grateful for from my childhood (even if it was unintentionally gendered) is how I learned to take care of myself and my surroundings. As a kid, I was expected to do the laundry, clean parts of the house, and even occasionally cook for myself. I grew up tagging along with my mother to the grocery store, understanding how to shop and plan meals, and seeing the work involved in keeping up our shared household. This training allowed me to take care of myself once I was out on my own, knowing how to do my own laundry, cook some basic meals, and keep my apartment (relatively) tidy. I took these experiences as normal until I started hearing from friends who were married to cisgender men who didn't know how to do these basic things and who sometimes seemed unwilling to learn.

Unequal household labor has become a standard conversation topic. With the popularity of Eve Rodsky's book *Fair Play* leading the charge, the conversation has also appeared in other places. Maggie Smith, in her memoir *You Could Make This Place Beautiful*, writes about how unequal household labor was one of the things that contributed to her divorce. She says, "It's too late to do anything about the inequity in my now-kaput marriage. But I made the list of tasks anyway. I wanted to see in black and white what I'd been doing in the marriage. Reader, I was going to show you the list, but I decided against it. You don't need the list. Looking at it, I thought, No wonder so many divorced men get remarried right away and so many divorced women stay on their own."

The ability of men to take care of themselves and contribute fairly to their household is a vital one. It's not just about cleaning or buying groceries. It's about the messages we've internalized, the things we believe about gender and responsibility, and it becomes an example of issues outside the household as well.

Let's start in the home. "But I didn't even see it," you say as your partner asks why you didn't carry the thing that was on the stairs upstairs when you went. She sighs, exasperated: "You stepped right over it!" You insist you didn't see it. Maybe this is how a lot of your household conversations seem to go. Your partner feeling frustrated that you didn't do something: pick up something, take out something, help out with something. You feeling frustrated because you didn't realize the thing needed to be done in the first place.

Many of us have internalized messages from pop culture, from our families of origin, or from other men that household work is unimportant or not men's responsibility. Beyond that, we've often internalized messages that say we can't really take care of ourselves. From the bumbling of sitcom dads to the memes about male Instacart shoppers, this notion of men's inability to step up is ingrained. Knowing how deep these beliefs go, we often take advantage of them. We use them, even unintentionally, to keep ourselves in positions of power and to make women subservient.

It's not just men who have internalized a message that we can't take care of ourselves. The messages about men in pop culture, in certain cultures and environments, and in the systems we live in teach women messages about men that are harmful to all of us. If women are taught that their partners can't take care of themselves, then they might overcompensate and try to do their partner's share too. Then when women get burnt out, they tend to blame themselves for not working hard enough. Or if women are taught that men can't control their sexual urges, they might be more likely to blame themselves if their partner cheats on them. Or to feel pressured to have sex even if they don't really want to or aren't in the mood, because women have been taught it's their responsibility to keep men happy or to cater to men's needs.

These beliefs, while on the surface seeming to affect only women negatively, also hurt us. We're taught we can't really contribute to our own household. We're not good nurturers, so we shouldn't try to comfort our crying children. We're not good at picking up after ourselves, so we shouldn't worry about the messy house. We don't notice when we need new clothing or when the towels are getting worn, so we place the responsibility for buying them on our partner.

We believe we're entitled to sex even if our partners aren't in the mood because we somehow "need it more." In doing this, we don't take any responsibility for our own desires, and we don't take any responsibility for the desires of our partners and what they might want or need or how to give them pleasure. We consider ourselves dependent on our impulses and not in control of them.

We believe it's impossible for men and women to have platonic relationships, and so we always manage to make our relationships with women weird. We rely on women to be our emotional supports even when we don't have any intention of returning the favor. We turn to them as surrogates instead of learning how to have hard conversations with our partners or our male friends.

More than anything, teachings and beliefs like this make us believe we are somehow separate from the other people (especially women) in our lives. We are somehow totally different. We share nothing in common. As the famous book says, men are from Mars, and women are from Venus, after all. These beliefs keep us locked into patterns that are no longer serving us. They're no longer serving our relationships.

And frankly, more and more women are tuned in to these patterns and are saying, "No, thanks. This just isn't worth it to me. I'd rather stay single. I'd rather not get married.

I'd rather have a house with friends, parent with friends, and do whatever I can to not have to 'raise' my partner."

What are you bringing to your relationship that someone can't get on their own? Are you additive, or are you a subtraction? In a world where women make their own money, buy their own houses, even have children on their own, why should they spend time on you? Some men don't want to confront these questions. They find ideas of their irrelevance insulting and blame women, feminism, liberals, whoever else they need to so they don't have to take responsibility for their own actions. These men never once seem to ask, "Am I worth the work I seem to require?"

But for other men, these questions cut us to the core because we're also asking them of ourselves; we're wondering where we fit, and we're worrying that we don't bring anything to the table. We feel like we're no longer necessary, and instead of figuring out how we might contribute again, we double down on outdated notions that no longer serve us or our potential partners. We sit at home blaming everyone else instead of asking what we might do to change things.

What might we add to a relationship? How might we step up to lighten the load of our partner? How do we add joy, fun, celebration to their lives instead of more work and hassle? Beyond two incomes and more material things, how do we contribute emotionally? Spiritually? Socially? Many of us have never had to ask ourselves these questions before, and so we're a little terrified to even consider it. What if we measure ourselves and find ourselves wanting? What if we realize it's not our partner's fault, it's not society's fault, it's not feminism's fault—it's *our* fault for not stepping up?

* * *

This is not an exclusively masculine problem, but for many women I've talked to (especially those who are partnered with men), it is indeed a problem that seems to more deeply affect women. It's so much of a problem that there have been scientific studies done about it. There is a whole field of language to describe it (*learned incompetence* is one phrase), and it's made its way into viral social media posts and memes. Men learning to actually show up in their households is a huge deal, not just to make their partners feel better or to lessen their mental load, but showing up in the household is also indicative that men are showing up in other areas of their lives too. They are working to undo ingrained patterns and behaviors that are leading to inequality.

If we learn to show up at home, we're learning to be better partners. We're learning to do labor that is often considered "women's work" and therefore considered by some to be not as important or beneath men. We're learning to examine and confront our entitlement (to being served, to having a home a certain way, etc.).

Starting with this step will radically transform our lives and relationships. It will start us on a journey of healing. I know that sounds like hyperbole, but I really believe it. If we can do this, we can start to turn the tide. Of course, it's not just about the dishes or the laundry; it's about showing up in new ways and examining why we weren't showing up in those ways before.

This is an invitation to step up, to lean into discomfort, to examine the ways we have contributed to our own issues by not being willing to look closely at ourselves.

You might wonder why your partner can't just tell you what they need. "Why do I have to read their mind?" The answer isn't quite as simple as you might think. It's not that your partner is playing a guessing game with you. It's that having to keep track of the entire household, a household of which you are a part, takes a mental load. So when you don't notice the dirty dishes in the sink or the basket that needs to go back upstairs or that milk is running low, you're not just *not* helping; you're actually putting more of a load on your partner. Multiply this by the home insurance and the milk, the laundry, kids' school lunches and registrations, sports teams and rehearsals, your work schedule, the night you invited your boss over for dinner, their own work schedule, what needs to be cleaned, what needs to be replaced, when the mortgage is due, and suddenly that's a whole lot to keep track of.

"I help when my partner asks me to!" Great! But they are still keeping track of everything that needs to be done. They need to ask you to do it (which sometimes can make it feel like they are managing or parenting you), and then they have to make sure it actually happens in case you forget. They're still managing all the work, even if you are helping. As Eve Rodsky says in *Fair Play*, "Having to remind your partner to do something doesn't take that something off your list. It adds to it. And what's more, reminding is often unfairly characterized as nagging. (Almost every man interviewed in connection with this project said nagging is what they hate most about being married, but they also admit that they wait for their wives to tell them what to do at home.)"

Rodsky recommends that each partner take ownership of certain tasks: "Ownership belongs to the person who first off remembers to plan, then plans, and then follows through on every aspect of executing the plan and completing the task without reminders." This is key: it's not just about doing part of the task; it's about doing the whole thing, doing it well, and doing it without reminders.

"Okay," I hear some of you say, "I'm convinced this is important, but when I told you I didn't see the thing on the steps, I really meant it. I didn't see it. How do I undo that?" And that's the real work.

Many men have been trained not to see. We've been trained not to know how to do things for ourselves. We've been trained to just let it be and it'll work itself out, but often what happens is our partners end up taking care of it.

This training is not always intentional (though sometimes it is). It might be that in your household, you were in charge of mowing the lawn on the weekends, and your sister was in charge of helping out with dinner. So you internalized an idea that lawns were for guys and dinner was for girls. So now, even though your household is more complex, you still mow the lawn on the weekends and consider that your contribution to the household.

It might be the case that you were never taught how to do certain things. You weren't taught how to meal plan or grocery shop. You didn't learn how to clean your house or do your laundry. No one ever taught you how to change a diaper or swaddle a baby or engage in imaginative play with a toddler. You might also, in addition to not being taught, have rarely or never seen a model of another man doing these things so you could learn by their example. All of these things might be true, and we can and should name them (and name the larger systems that see these things as unnecessary for boys to learn) while also not continuing to use them as an excuse to let us off the hook or to keep us from learning how to do them now.

There also might be a difference in comfortability with certain standards in your household. You might be just fine with piles of laundry in the bedroom or with eating a frozen pizza three nights in a row. You might not understand what the big deal is about a pristine living room or making sure the toddlers' clothes match when all you're doing is going to the playground. You might need to open up a conversation with your spouse, as Eve Rodsky suggests in *Fair Play*, to get clear on shared standards for certain activities. She recommends "having a collaborative discussion about what is reasonable in your own home." This might also be a place where understanding the different standards women are held to when it comes to cleanliness and children makes you see things differently. The way our culture is currently set up, men will often get applauded for doing the bare minimum, especially when it comes to caring for their children, but if a woman shows up to the playground with a kid in mismatched clothing, she might be labeled a bad mother, neglectful, or worse. Getting on the same page as your partner as to what matters to both of you, where there are areas of compromise, and where there are nonnegotiables will lead to less stress and tension overall.

The reality is that partners can work out all sorts of solutions to make their households run smoothly. Maybe you and your partner both work full-time jobs. You don't mind doing the laundry, and your partner loves to fold, so you split the chore like that, and every week, it gets done. Or maybe one of you loves to cook, and the other gets giddy about the idea of a super clean floor, and so you split those tasks. And sometimes maybe those things break down along traditionally gendered lines. I'm not saying that's a bad thing, that you can't mow the lawn if you really love to do it or that your partner shouldn't ever do the dishes. I am saying that if you're not having a conversation about these tasks, if you're not being intentional about who's doing what, if you're not in agreement about what's getting done, and when, and by whom—then you're much more likely to end up with a partner who feels taken advantage of and bitter.

Rodsky writes in her book, "What's fair is not always equal and what is equal is not always fair, so don't expect a 50/50 split. The goal of Fair Play is equity, not equality."

* * *

Many of us think it's already too late. Patterns are already set. There's nothing that can be done. We've already relinquished any stake we have in being active in our home life, and so we don't course-correct. Or we try once, and it doesn't work, so we tell ourselves it's not worth trying again. Then we let things continue to wander on the way they've been going, and we're suddenly shocked when our kids want nothing to do with us or our partner files for divorce. We assumed that everyone else was operating on the same status quo we were, and the jolt into a new reality throws us for a loop. But we could have intervened earlier. We could have paid attention to what wasn't working. We could have asked for help or said how we were feeling or tried to do something differently.

It's this unreflective willingness to operate on the status quo that gets so many of us into situations that feel untenable to us and to those around us. Many men tend to go with the flow until the flow doesn't work for the people around them, and then they are forced to change. But what if we could change without being forced? What if we were self-aware enough to realize that things weren't working the way we wanted them to? What if we could interrupt our own patterns when we realized they had stopped working for us and for those around us? What if we changed before the damage is too much?

* * *

What about outside your immediate household? Where else do these patterns come into play? When it comes to your extended family, who organizes the gifts for your parents for

Christmas? Do you assume that your mother or sister will host the family gathering or plan all the details and just let you know what to bring?

Let's also consider our offices and work environments. My wife told me a story about working as an executive assistant at a progressive seminary. In the office, they had a shared kitchen space. She noted that it was exclusively men who left their dirty dishes in the sink when they were done eating. Maybe these men intended to come back and clean them up later, maybe they didn't think they needed to be responsible, or maybe they just assumed someone else would do it, but it was telling to my wife that it was never the women who left behind their dishes.

Or consider the office birthday celebrations. Whose responsibility is it to remember the birthdays, to get the card, to buy the treats? Do you assume that someone else will take care of it, or do you offer to be a part of the rotation making sure everyone gets recognized?

There are also the many stories told of the assumption that women will be the notetakers in all meetings, even when they have a higher title than men in the room. The idea that taking notes is somehow feminine work, or beneath the attention of men, enforces gendered dynamics in the workplace.

Paying attention to all the places where these dynamics play out is vital to correcting them. We can't expect people to ask us to step up; we must do it on our own.

We can start by noticing. Then taking an active role in the upkeep of our household and with our children is one of the best ways we can make our partners feel like they are indeed our partners and not our parent.

For those of us in same-gender relationships or who are unpacking our own upbringings and socialization as trans folks, we might need to examine which ideas we've internalized about who does what or how gendered expectations come into play in our relationships. As a trans man, I've learned to pay closer attention to where there might be gendered expectations in my own relationships. As someone married to a woman, I don't want to recreate systems of inequality in our household. It means being extra vigilant about the assumptions I might be making about what our roles are. Where are the places I might be sliding into a gendered expectation, even accidentally? How can I open up lines of communication with my partner so that neither one of us feels taken advantage of or overworked in our shared life together?

Certainly, there are times in our lives when one partner has a heavier load than another, a busy season of travel or a year-end push at work. Or seasons of life when one partner has more bandwidth than another. One person stepping up to do more at home during those times is natural. What we need to watch out for is unspoken assumptions about what's happening in our households and whose responsibility it is to do what.

For many men, we need to unlearn the incompetence we've inherited. We've learned that incompetence works for us. If we don't know how to do things and it will take our partner a long time to explain or teach us, we know they'll just do it themselves. If we do something badly and they have to redo it, they probably won't ask us again. We might not necessarily mean to make things harder for our partners, but when we do things poorly (or don't learn how on our own), we load that burden onto our partner. If we want to show up differently and have a better relationship, we have to unlearn these behaviors.

Unlearning incompetence first requires paying attention. Studies show that men often think they are doing equal housework, while women disagree. We need to begin by paying attention to not only what we do around the house but also how we're doing it. Are we only doing it when asked? Is our partner the one who manages everything, and we simply "help out"? If so, we need to figure out how we can take some of the load off of our partner (and we have to figure it out on our own, not simply by asking them to delegate tasks to us). What would it look like to enter into a relationship with no expectations based on gender, where you could decide, as a unit, how you were going to split household responsibilities, pay for things, care for your pets and/or your children, and make decisions? Wouldn't it be a relief? Approach these things as a conversation to find out what would work best for you.

Unlearning our incompetence will also mean getting comfortable with discomfort. We might wander lost around the grocery store for a while, feeling silly that we need to double back to find something we missed the first time through.

We might have to watch videos about how to use our appliances or realize it takes us longer to do something than we think it should because we're still learning how to do it. We might feel awkward as we try to learn new skills. Sitting with our discomfort and learning to do it anyway is part of this process. Just as we wouldn't expect to learn a new sport or musical instrument the first time we tried, we also need to understand that learning how to do household tasks might take time and feel difficult and frustrating at first.

Maybe you start by declaring Saturday your day. It's your day to prepare all the meals, which also means figuring out what ingredients you'll need and making a plan for purchasing those ingredients, and it's your day to plan the activities and get the kids ready. Or you declare one room of the house to be your responsibility, and you clean it every day (with a deep clean on the weekends).

You could start to really look at all the work your partner does throughout the week—meal planning, outfit prepping, laundry—and seeing what you might be able to take off their plate. Could you start to do the household's laundry? Or put it away? Could you plan and cook three meals a week and also go shopping for those meals?

If you've never had a conversation with your partner about how household tasks are split up, that's a good place to start. If you're not in a practice of regularly communicating with your partner about the house and the kids, setting up a weekly check-in will help. Come to this check-in prepared to tell your partner what you have going on this upcoming week, anything that's out of the ordinary, and how you plan to participate in the household. Allow your partner to do the same and see if there are any days or times when something might be falling through the cracks. It's better to be prepared for those things and be able to make a plan together than for you to be assuming that your partner will just handle it.

Part of this work might be learning how to do some things you've never had to do before. Do you know how all of the appliances in your household work? Do you know how to use the washer and dryer? Or run the dishwasher? (These might seem like silly questions to some of you, but the number of men I've seen who don't know how to do their own laundry or even cook a simple meal is quite high.) Are there a couple of recipes you can make—not just heating up something in a box but actually cooking some ingredients?

This isn't just for men who are married or partnered. All men could stand to use some skill-building in the areas of our lives that relate to health and home. Learning how to do things that we weren't taught to do is a way of not only challenging social norms but also showing up for ourselves. We should be able to feed ourselves well, take care of our clothing and households, and know how to take care of children (even if we choose not to parent). Beyond learning the basics, these areas of our life can lead to better health outcomes, a calmer mind, and deeper relationships.

If you're a parent, you might have to do some work to learn what's happening in your children's lives: Do you know what goes in your children's lunches? The names of their teachers?

Who their doctors are? Do you know where their medical records are kept?

Even more than tasks, this work requires us to look deeply at the assumptions we make about our households and our place in them. What does it mean to be a partner to your spouse? What does it mean to show up fully to your spouse and children? What does it mean to be active in their lives? How can you take a larger role in your family's life?

What is keeping you from stepping up in that way? Are you worried you'll get it wrong? Are you worried you're not wanted? Do you feel like it's not your job because of other things you do to contribute?

Learning to show up in our households as competent and equal partners will shift so much. It will improve our relationships with our partners and our children. It will reduce the overall stress of the household.

As we learn to contribute to not only our households but also our workplaces, we will feel the joy of adding value into the places where we spend our time. If we've been worried about feeling like we don't matter, the best place to start is to add value and contribute where we are. This is a step on the path to better masculinity, for us and for those we love.

CHAPTER FIVE

Accessing More Emotions

Early in my transition, I was taking the subway to seminary, as I did most days. In New York, you learn the rhythm of the cars and how, by getting in a certain car, you can save yourself steps when you get off at your station. I was changing trains to get on the one that would take me to the seminary and shuffling along the crowded platform to get into the car I needed to get into. I had big headphones on and was focused on getting through the crowd. Without meaning to, I made and held eye contact with a man heading toward me. I don't know what it was—my angry-looking resting face, the fact that I held his eyes too long, or the fact that I was moving toward him quickly—but he did that upper body gesture that's like "come at me." I hurriedly dropped my eyes and steered clear, but I got on the train car feeling shaky. I felt like

I had come close to violence, but I didn't understand why. Why was making eye contact with a stranger so threatening? It was a new experience, one I had never had before. I felt both grateful to have been gendered correctly in that moment and also worried. Is this what it means to be a man? The constant threat of violence? Never being able to make eye contact unless you're also ready for a fight?

Years later, on another means of public transportation (this time a bus), I was standing toward the front because there were no seats. I had, once again, big headphones on and was listening to music. I wasn't looking at anyone or anything, tired after a long day of work. I happened to notice the man across from me saying something, but I couldn't hear him because I had music playing. I was a little annoyed to be spoken to (headphones should be the universal symbol for "please don't talk to me"), but I pulled one of the earpieces to the side and said "What?" Immediately the man was ready to fight: "Oh, you wanna fight? You wanna fight?" I replied, "No. I just didn't hear you." But he was uninterested in my response. So I simply put my headphones back on and refused to engage more, thankful, for once, that the bus was crowded and hoping it would keep this man from throwing a punch.

I remain slightly baffled by these incidents. The readiness with which these men were ready to throw down with a complete stranger over perceived slights such as eye contact and not hearing a question. How do you explain things like this? I'd be inclined to say they were isolated experiences, but I'm honestly not sure. And hearing the stories of women catcalled, pestered, and harassed in public by strangers also leads me to believe these stories aren't rare. What is it about our shared spaces that enable men to behave like this?

Another story: I was with a group of friends out dancing. It was the end of the night, and the bar was closing down. We sprawled out onto the street, still yelling because our ears were fuzzy from the pounding bass. We were a little tipsy and very sweaty and enjoying each other's company. There were others crowded on the curb waiting for Ubers and Lyfts or just not quite ready to go home yet. People were doing their complicated dances of trying to not go home alone. I was with my friends, waiting for our ride, when suddenly a fight broke out. A group of men were brawling, and I realized my friends' proximity to the street meant that if these guys didn't knock it off, my friends would be in danger. So I reached into the mix of the fight, not to join in but to restrain the men who were fighting. Suddenly I found myself pushed against a wall with someone's arm across my throat. It was their friends fighting, and they were mad that I intervened.

My friend Alison jokingly yelled at the men for fighting and me for getting involved, "The damn testosterone! It's all the testosterone!" It was as if she believed it was my maleness that had caused me to leap into the fray. I was simply concerned with keeping my friends safe. I had no interest in fighting. I didn't want *them* to be fighting. I wanted every one of us to get home safely that night. In that moment, I wasn't thinking about violence; I was thinking about protection.

The fact that Alison wanted to blame it all on testosterone isn't unique to her. Many people over the years have blamed testosterone for all sorts of things. It's one of the easiest things to blame for men's recklessness, risk-taking, and willingness to fight, and it takes away men's responsibility for their own actions and behaviors.

Years later after a theatre performance, I was standing in the lobby with a woman and another man. She was commenting about how she felt leaving the theatre late at night and being super aware of where her car was parked, who was around, making sure she was holding her keys, and so on. When she had gotten to the venue earlier, she made sure to park under a streetlight so her car would be in the light on her way out. She asked the two of us, "Do you think about that when you leave at night?" The other guy immediately said, "No. I just go." But I couldn't say that. I do, indeed, think about things like that. I, too, sometimes walk with my keys clenched in my fist. I pay attention to the sound of steps behind me when I'm walking down the street at night. I check the car before getting into it.

My experiences as a man are shaped by my growing up assumed female. They are also shaped by intimately knowing the statistics about violence toward transgender people. Hell, we trans folks have a day of remembrance every single year to pay tribute to those who have been murdered in the past calendar year. Every single year there are more names on the list than the year before. While I know that transgender women of color are the ones most at risk for violence, I also know that none of us is immune.

After a lifetime spent mostly around women, I struggle to be in men's-only spaces. I don't know how to talk to men. I'm still learning the codes of what's acceptable and what's not. The constant drip of shallow conversations about sports and the weather is exhausting. I want to go deeper, but I'm not always sure how.

Then there are the spaces where I worry I'm at risk of violence: the men's bathroom, the locker room at the gym, going shirtless at the pool. Are people looking at my body? Wondering about my scars? Clocking me as trans? If they do clock me as trans, will I be safe?

In rooms of mixed genders, I find myself drawn to the women for conversation. I watch as the other men stick to the periphery, or tend the grill, or focus on their food.

This seems to be a trend, though: Men turn to women when they want to have conversations about their feelings, when they want emotional support, when they want to be listened to. They turn to women because they can't seem to reach out to the men in their lives; they can't seem to figure out how to bridge that chasm. So women become the bearers of men's emotional burdens because we're unable to bear them for each other.

It feels risky to go first. It feels risky to invite someone into that emotional space. What if they don't want to go there? Or worse, what if they laugh at me or make fun of me? What if they reject me?

We haven't been taught to deal with emotional rejection. For as strong as we've been told men are, studies are now showing that hardship affects men more deeply. Men, frankly, are not very resilient. We feel it. We see it on the news and the internet. Men having meltdowns over the smallest things. Men turning to violence because they feel rejected. Sure, we code it as being "disrespected," but the reality is we feel hurt. We feel ashamed. We feel rejected, and so we lash out. We have been taught the only response we have available to us is violence. That's how we take control, that's how we seize back power, it's how we make ourselves feel better.

This turn toward violence and hostility keeps us locked into cycles that are killing us. It separates us from society (by landing us in prison), it separates us from our families and children (either legally or because they feel unsafe with us), it separates us from connection (because we're always caught in this cycle of needing to defend our honor), and it keeps us unhealthy (health problems, mental problems, suicide when the violence turns inward). Yet many of us don't know how to break these cycles. We're afraid to break them because what if we try something new, and it doesn't work?

What happens when you've been taught you are only allowed to have one emotion? You translate every single feeling into that one emotion. For many men, the only thing we've been taught we're allowed to feel is anger. This is especially dangerous when it comes to emotional interactions with others. We are seeing an epidemic of rage, especially in the United States, in men.

Consider the following scenario: A young man, feeling fear about his future job prospects, feeling sadness about his lack of relationships, feeling lonely, doesn't know how to name or sit with any of those emotions. He instead takes all of those things and pushes them into a ball of rage. He feeds himself on a steady drip of news and other media that tells him other people are to blame for everything that's going wrong in his life. He doesn't know where to put all of the things he's feeling or how to deal with them in a healthy way, and so he acts it out on the people closest to him. At first maybe he's just testy with people in his family (especially the women or those younger and smaller than he is). He might say demeaning things or lash out in anger. Maybe he punches a wall or throws his video game controller. After a while, maybe this anger turns to violence toward the people in his household. Maybe he's violent toward someone he's dating. Maybe he has a gun and goes into a school or a movie theater or a concert and acts out his rage on the people around him. He feels justified in doing it, making other people hurt the way he's been hurt.

This isn't, at all, to excuse this behavior. Or even to try to generate empathy for people who choose to be violent toward others. Instead, it's a wake-up call to men to start to deal with our emotions and to intervene in the rage and anger of other men. The problem isn't the woman who might reject the advances of this young man. The problem isn't women or people from other countries or other races (because let's be clear, it's almost always white men who choose to enact their violence on large groups of people) taking the job he thinks should belong to him. The fault isn't "the culture," which is "trying to emasculate" him—as so many alt-right person-alities claim. The problem is with his anger and how he's choosing to express it. He makes his problem our problem.

The reason it's on men, on us, to interrupt this behavior is because for too long we've excused it. We've created the systems that have allowed young men to be violent. We've created the atmospheres that keep them from knowing how to deal with their feelings. We've created the culture that keeps men isolated and afraid. We've done this every time we've shamed a boy for expressing his emotions by telling him "boys don't cry" or that he needs to "man up." When we let boys off the hook when they hit someone or throw something, when we excuse their anger and rage instead of helping them figure out what's underneath it, when we show boys that anger is the only emotion available to them, we reinforce these behaviors.

＊　＊　＊

Let's talk about fear. Men aren't supposed to be afraid. We're not supposed to show fear. We're not supposed to admit when we feel uneasy or uncertain. If I were to say to you that most men are terrified most of the time, your immediate response is probably going to be bluster. "I'm not afraid! What are you talking about?"

Now let's talk about rage. When you or men you know feel affronted or threatened, what do they do? They often fly into a rage.

I know, for me, rage often masks either pain or fear. This is a silly example, but if I'm working at home, and I've got my noise-canceling headphones on, and my wife comes up behind me and startles me, I often get mad. I don't fly into a rage or yell, but internally I'm angry. Why? Because I was afraid. Because in that moment, I felt vulnerable. I felt uncomfortable. I don't like being snuck up on.

I grew up in a rural area. The summers of my childhood were marked by running barefoot through the yard, climbing trees, catching frogs in the backyard creek, and generally being filthy. One day, I was playing with my aunts (who were close to my age). I was barefoot and not paying attention, and I stepped on a board that had a nail sticking out of it. The nail went right into my foot, all the way in. In the process of lifting another piece of wood up and trying to free my foot, something also bonked me on the head. Pain on top of pain. I remember pulling my foot free of the nail and not wanting anyone to touch me. They tried to comfort me, and I lashed out. I was so overwhelmed with pain and fear that I couldn't accept comfort. But I also couldn't express how afraid and in pain I was. The only emotion I had access to was anger. A small child in pain yelling is a whole lot different from a grown man yelling. The emotional response is the same, but the impact is different.

There are so many examples of men screaming, frothing at the mouth in anger over something. Yes, some of those men are just angry, driven by rage and hatred. I'm not denying that or trying to mitigate the impact. But I do think that behind the anger in some men is simply a deep sense of fear. Fear that the world is changing, and there's no place for them in it anymore. Fear they're being left behind. Fear that all of the things they believe they were promised—good jobs, pension plans, retirement, children to take care of them in their old age—are rapidly disappearing, and they don't know what to do about it. Fear that they don't know how to exist in this new world, that if the things they thought were true aren't true anymore, then they don't know what to do or how to be.

And then there's the pain: Pain that we were lied to. Pain that we were promised something false. Pain that the ways we've been living have hurt other people, even people we deeply love. We feel pain that we've been deprived of another way of being. We feel pain that we've followed all the rules, and it's still not enough.

We are deeply afraid and deeply in pain. But we haven't been taught or encouraged to express fear or pain. And so we rage. We blame other communities, we blame the media, we blame "wokeness," we blame anything and everyone so that we don't have to feel our fear. So we don't have to feel our immense pain. It's easier to lash out. We've been trained to lash out. We've been taught that it's manly to lash out.

Or we shut down. We shove all of that fear and pain so deep inside that it can't touch us. Except it does. It touches every part of our life, and because it's shoved so deeply, when the tendrils bubble out, they come out as rage or at inappropriate times. We fly off the handle at the slightest inconvenience.

When we try to express the pain we're feeling or the struggles we face, we feel (or we're outright told) that we're taking away from the pain of other people who have it worse. This is why it's so crucial for us to learn how to express our emotions, to do so in spaces with other men, and to do it in a way that pays attention to the interconnectedness of systems of injustice and to the ways that we've historically participated in those systems.

Let's say you're experiencing a hard emotion. You're at work, and your boss tells you you're being passed up for the promotion you applied for. Your first impulse is to say you're angry. And anger is probably a part of it. Don't deny that part. You can start there, but don't stop there. Try to sit with this feeling. What else is in there? Are you worried or afraid about what this means for your family? Are you afraid that you'll be at risk in the next round of layoffs? Are you hurt that your boss doesn't see your value to the company? Or that your boss chose someone over you? Is your pride feeling wounded because you thought you were a shoo-in for this new position? Are you feeling embarrassed because you feel like you can't quite keep up?

Our inability to deal with our fear (or to simply call it *anger* and act it out) often leads us toward violence.

These two things, anger and violence, have come to define masculinity for a lot of people, but if these are the only options you feel you have available to you, of course you're going to lean on them.

* * *

Early in my transition, I became obsessed with the idea of the military and combat. It started with watching *Band of Brothers*, the HBO miniseries about Easy Company of the 42nd Airborne in World War II. I was captivated by the heartbreaking and beautifully produced series following the men in this company from their training all the way through to the end of the war. As I watched, I was, of course, horrified by the brutality of war. Horrified by the pettiness of some of the men in charge. But I was also taken with the connections between these men. The way they took care of one another, the way they grieved for one another, the way they talked about fighting not for freedom or for lofty goals but for the man in the foxhole with them.

I began to read other military memoirs, one after the other. I read about World War II and the wars in Iraq and Afghanistan. I read about young men (barely even men) signing up and going through training and coming back changed. I read memoirs of chaplains. I became a little bit obsessed, honestly. I was reaching for something I wasn't quite sure how to articulate. I wanted my own band of brothers. I wanted to connect deeply with other men in a way I didn't see happening with the men around me. There was something about the way the men who had faced battle together talked that I was hungry for. Looking back, I can say I was naïve. I can say my desire was ill-placed, but there was something about those friendships.

I bought myself a military-issue backpack. I bought a box of MREs (meals ready-to-eat) off of eBay and started taking those for my lunch. When people asked why I was doing this, I told them it was convenient (and they honestly are), but it was also because I wanted to know what it was like to eat like people in the military. I bought combat boots and camo pants. I'm sure I looked ridiculous. I know some of my classmates and friends thought I was being absurd, but I was striving for something. In these military memoirs, I saw men who were being honest about their fears, men who were connected deeply to other men, men who were trying to be a part of something bigger than they were. In these documentaries and in the war photos by Tim Herrington, Sebastian Junger, and others, I saw men being tender with one another. Holding each other in grief or in sleep or after years apart. There was a tenderness there, and it was earned by all they had been through together. I wanted that.

I tried to enroll in the US Navy as a chaplain, but I couldn't even get past the first conversation because I was transgender. Automatically, I was disqualified.

It wasn't that I glorified the military—in fact, I had quite complex feelings about the military. I wasn't glamorizing war. But I did want to be a part of something that was bigger than me. I wanted to be connected deeply with other men. And when I saw that the vast majority of military chaplains were theologically and politically conservative, I did feel like I could add a different and much-needed perspective to people of faith who needed someone progressive in their theology.

I remember trying to explain the pull I felt to one of my friends. The military felt like the only place where I could find the closeness with other men that I longed for, the commitment to a larger mission, the testing of myself in violence or its aftermath. It's telling that when I looked to places for male camaraderie and larger mission, the military seemed not only *one* of the only places it was happening; it also seemed like one of the most accessible. What does that say about us as a society?

It's not that dissimilar from the way some men will say you're not really a man until you've learned how to throw (and take) a punch. Or how hazing gets passed down in sports teams, with the idea that learning to accept violence done to you makes you stronger and more masculine. Andrew Reiner, in his book *Better Boys, Better Men*, talks about hazing in this way: "It's lauded as 'tradition' because this designation gives the men who have endured suffering the right to inflict their shame and psychic pain on younger, more vulnerable men. It's a sanctioned form of sadism, really, which perpetuates the deeply held belief that someone else must also pay when a man is forced to suffer." We lean on violence because it's what we were taught. We were taught that being violent and bearing up under violence is what proves you're a man.

We have to unlearn anger and violence as our go-to modes of being. We have to learn how to feel our fear. We have to learn how to feel our pain. We have to deal with it, so we don't keep acting it out on other people.

The ideas that the only masculine emotion is rage, that the only way to express pain is through violence, that men are allowed to hit things but not to cry, to scream but not to wail, to attack but not to tend—these are all things we need to counter in order to experience our full humanity and find freedom.

We need to find places of camaraderie that aren't centered on violence and brutality, finding other places and ways to connect with one another, to develop deep intimacy, and to cultivate companionship.

* * *

How do we start to move away from only being able to express anger and violence? The first thing we need to learn to do is name what's actually happening inside ourselves. When we've lived for so long divorced from our feelings or feeling like we're only allowed to express anger, then of course that's what we experience. It's the old "if the only tool you have is a hammer, then everything looks like a nail" trope lived out in our emotions. We need to start to have a larger vocabulary for our own emotional landscape.

This isn't touchy-feely BS; this is about awareness and precision of language. When we have a better sense of what's actually happening inside of us, we become aware of a larger range of possibilities to deal with it.

My friend Brian has a "feelings list." It's a giant list of words that name various feelings. Things like *joy, bliss, engaged, indifferent, useless, resigned, satisfied, free, worthy, strong*—the list goes on and on. The difference between *joy* and *bliss* or *worthy* and *strong* might not seem like it matters much at first, but the more you dive into these words and connect them to your actual states of being, the more you can understand what's happening inside of you.

You're allowed to be curious about your emotions and what you're feeling. Many of us haven't been taught that we're allowed curiosity (or how to nurture it), but it's the first step to being in control of your emotional self. Control isn't about tamping down our emotions; it's about choosing how we respond to them. So next time you feel frustrated or hurt, you can make a choice about your response (to communicate it, to step away for a while) instead of allowing your emotions to control you (where you hurt someone back or lash out in violence).

Having more access to your interior life also gives you more access to behaviors and choices. Where once everything looked like a nail, now you can see that there are nails and screws and hooks and suction cups and all sorts of ways to solve problems.

As we become more in tune with what we're experiencing, better able to name our emotions and our feelings, next we learn to pause before responding. Instead of lashing out, throwing a punch, jumping into the fray, we can take a beat and assess a better course of action. Maybe the best thing to do in a certain situation is to jump in—but maybe it's to step back, to de-escalate, to wait a minute. Maybe we can talk out a situation. Maybe we can walk away. Maybe there are other options we couldn't even see before.

Then we start to uncover other ways to be connected to other people and to connect with ourselves. What does it look like to have camaraderie outside of battle or the gym or mixed martial arts (MMA)? How might we cultivate intimacy without fear or anxiety? What would it look like to hug our friends more often or put an arm around another guy?

We begin to find other ways of proving ourselves to ourselves, knowing our masculinity isn't found in our willingness and ability to do violence. We can let others (and ourselves) off the hook of proving our toughness (more about being tough in the next chapter) and can simply be ourselves. As we start to let down our guard, we'll find new ways to connect with other men that go deeper and feel safer than what is currently available to us. We'll be able to show up to these encounters as our full selves, not having to prove anything to anyone.

CHAPTER SIX

Tough Guys Don't Win

It took me a long time to find language for my identity. Growing up as I did in a rural community, anchored to a conservative evangelical church, homeschooled through all of high school, there wasn't a lot of exposure to "alternative" identities. You were a man, or you were a woman, and you were straight. There weren't other options.

There were a few outliers—the single missionary woman, the older bachelor—but those were few and far between. My existence outside of traditional gender roles perplexed and agitated people. From the time I was very young, I wore a baseball cap everywhere. People would ask why I always wore it, and I would tell them, simply, that I liked it. They all commented on the fact that I would grow out of it, even as their words were tinged with some anxiety about when that would happen. As the years rolled by and that hat stayed firmly on my head, I could sense their nervousness increasing.

Then came the wars over my hair. I wanted to cut it short, but my mom wanted me to keep it long. Finally, a compromise: I could cut it, but I wasn't allowed to shave the back because that was "for boys." I was happy to have my hair shorter, even if it did mean I was basically rocking a mullet. There were battles over my desire to shop in the boys' section, my refusal to wear dresses and skirts, my extra-baggy clothing. I told myself (and everyone else) I was just being modest, but the reality is something felt wrong and off in my body. The ease I had felt as a child was disappearing as my chest grew larger and I was being expected to behave differently, more in line with the woman everyone thought I was becoming. Ever since puberty, I had been miserable, but I kept assuming the feelings would pass. I would eventually grow into my skin. That's what happened to everyone, right? Puberty was weird, but then you survived it and became yourself.

When I realized I was primarily attracted to women, I thought I must be gay, and I figured that explained my desire to have short hair and wear baggy clothes. Ellen DeGeneres was pretty much the only role model I had. But even as I started to get more comfortable in my sexuality, there was still something that didn't feel right. I still didn't like my body. I still didn't feel comfortable in tight clothing or anything that highlighted curves I might have. I didn't always feel like I fit into women's-only spaces (even as I was in them more and more), and I was uncomfortable with feminine language when it was used to describe me.

I learned more about feminism and queer spaces, I learned about the spectrum of identity, and I tried on new words to see if any of them fit. I called myself *genderqueer* (this was before *nonbinary* was a popular term and identity). I said I was *gender fucking.* Those words took some of the pressure off, but there was still something not right. Every time someone said I was a lesbian, I felt this tinge of *ugh.* Not because there was anything wrong with that word, but it just didn't feel like *me.* I called myself *gay,* and that felt better. Later I would identify as queer, which felt the most like home. But still there was something off. Not quite right. I kind of theoretically knew that transgender people existed, but at this point, I didn't think I had met anyone who identified that way. This was in 2007 and 2008. There were no television shows featuring transgender people. We didn't have anyone like Elliot Page or Laverne Cox to look up to. The representations we had in the media were Max on *The L Word*, who, as soon as he started to transition, turned into a monster filled with rage and violence. I definitely knew I didn't want to be like that.

* * *

It was my partner at the time who asked, "Do you think you might be trans?" I shut her down. I couldn't envision a future for myself as transgender. It was hard enough to come out as gay. I was still struggling to find my place in my family and my church as an out gay person. I thought transitioning would be a bridge too far. No one would understand me. No one would accept me. Besides, I didn't think I was a man.

That's what I told myself at the time. But I never really stopped to ask myself what being a man would feel like.

I did what nerds like me always do: I reached for books. I found whatever memoirs of transgender men I could get my hands on. Many of them had come out over a decade before. They were hard to track down. I had to look for used copies on Amazon and eBay, waiting until they arrived, slightly battered, on my doorstep. In these memoirs, I found echoes of Max from *The L Word*: the same type of hypermasculinity, the same emphasis on how testosterone made the authors angrier and quicker to violence. Again, I was put off. This wasn't the type of man I wanted to be. This wasn't the type of *person* I wanted to be. If this was what it meant to be a man, then maybe I wasn't one.

I read these stories hoping there would be such a clear, singular transgender male story that I could say, "Yes, that's me!" But I didn't find it, which made me doubt myself.

Now I know more about why these memoirs followed the patterns they did. In the first several decades of transgender medical care, getting access to care meant convincing a series of cisgender doctors that you were really who you said you were. You had to get a diagnosis of gender identity disorder in order to get any medical treatment. Transgender people learned fairly quickly that cisgender doctors had their own biases against and around gender identity and what it was that made someone trans. So transgender people learned the scripts to say that would allow them access to the care they knew they needed. They learned how to tell their life story in such a way that a cisgender person could hear it and empathize with them. So began the narratives of "I always hated dresses" and "I've always known I was a boy." Narratives that fit. Narratives that opened doors.

I didn't exactly see myself in those narratives. I never told anyone I was a boy because I didn't know it was an option. Never mind the fact that as an elementary schooler, I gave myself a boy's name as a "play name." Never mind the fact that in every story I told about myself to fall asleep at night, I would say I was a boy (either born a boy or I had somehow magically become one). But I also played with dolls and had Barbies and liked to play school. I sometimes wore dresses as a small kid and didn't hate them.

After all, there was a lot of pressure on me to *not* be trans. I was married to a woman who identified as a lesbian. I was in a queer community that was heavily invested in women's spaces. I was in a religious community that had barely made peace with LGB folks, and so I knew being trans was going to be a stretch, even for the most progressive people. I also looked around the world and didn't see a lot of spaces for trans folks. It would be easier for me to figure out how to be a woman than it would be to transition.

But even without a lot of models of healthy masculinity, once the idea was opened up that I might be transgender, that I might be a man, there was something I couldn't shake. I thought about it all the time. Was this who I was?

I decided to try on the identity at first. I bought a binder to make my chest flatter, and I bought a device that allowed me to feel I had a bulge in my pants. I remember pulling these things out of the package and feeling both embarrassed and intrigued. Was this really going to make me feel better? Turns out the answer was *yes*. The binder especially. I put that on and slipped a T-shirt over it and rushed to the mirror. This was what my body could look like? No. This was what my body *should* look like. All those years of angst suddenly made sense. My body wasn't as it was supposed to be.

I told a couple of friends I thought I might be trans. Their response? "Um, of course you are." *Oh.* They saw in me what I was barely able to admit about myself.

I reached out to a gender therapist and made an appointment. As we started meeting and talking, I realized all of my fears about transitioning weren't about whether or not I was a man, they were about what other people would think. How would this affect my marriage? My relationship with my family? My job search? One day in therapy, I realized that even if I lost everything, even if transitioning cost me every relationship in my life, my job, my stability, I had to do it. This was who I was. I was a man. I needed to live as myself.

I started the process of medically transitioning, reaching out to doctors, getting letters from psychologists, getting blood tests, figuring out the financials. I started testosterone and immediately felt better. I felt a sense of peace that I was making the right decision. Even though the hormones would take time to have a visible effect, it brought me calm to know I was taking concrete steps to align my inner world and my outer reality.

At this time, there were three surgeons in the United States who performed chest surgeries on trans men. *Three.* In the whole country. So I raised money and made plans and figured out how to get the appointment and travel hours and hours away in order to get this surgery. Insurance didn't cover it, so I had to pay for the surgery in cash as well as stay in a strange city for a week recovering in a hotel. But the moment I saw my new chest, the moment I saw my chest as it always should have been, I began to come home to my body in a new way, and I knew all of this was worth it.

I was still left with the looming question, though: What did it mean to be a man? I mean, I knew I was one, in my body and in my bones, but I didn't know what that meant for how I was out in the world. It felt like everyone else had been given some kind of manual, and I was left off the receiving list. (I would later learn that almost every man feels this way, like everyone else got the memo, and they didn't.) I was floundering. I felt right for the first time, but I still didn't know how to act.

I had to relearn my body. Take off all the ways of being that I had internalized because they helped me blend in or feel safe. And it was everything, right? It wasn't just how I moved my arms or how I sat. It was also how I spoke and what words I used; it was how I walked down the street and how I interacted with other people.

At the time, LiveJournal was a huge resource for transgender men. There were communities of people who shared their journeys on testosterone and how to navigate the medical system. They shared their surgery and recovery stories. They comforted one another when families wouldn't use a person's right name or pronouns or when a beloved partner left because they couldn't handle the transition. Guys also turned to these communities to figure out how to navigate life as men. There were all sorts of "passing" tips. Being perceived as the gender we are was a high priority, and we realized there were certain things that were likely to give us away, especially early in our medical transitions. There were tips on what kind of shirts to wear to hide your binder or minimize the flair of your hips, tips on how to lower your voice and pay attention to the upspeak at the end of your sentences, tips on how to sit in a chair and how to shake hands—all of these things that we had to relearn after years of being socialized as and treated as women. Even if we never identified that way (or did because we didn't know there was anything that was a better fit), we internalized ways of being that helped us move through the world. Those same ways of being were no longer serving us and needed to be jettisoned.

This idea, though, that masculinity is all in the acting of it doesn't tell the whole story. Sure, there are the unspoken rules of socialization and embodiment (like don't talk in the men's restroom, keep your eyes on the floor, and don't smile), but the idea that masculinity is only in what you do and how you carry your body isn't everything. Once I was being perceived more and more often correctly as male, I had other questions. Okay, now I'm a man. What does that mean? This was the existential question. The soul question.

What does it mean to be a man? Not just what does a man's body look like and what does a man sound like, but what, actually, is a man?

Once again I turned to books and pop culture to try to answer this question. I also turned into a keen observer of the men around me. Trying to watch and see what made them tick. Paying attention to how they spoke to one another and how they spoke to me. Paying attention to how they treated me and how it was different from the ways they treated me before. I was like a sociologist trying to uncover and understand the patterns.

At first, I wanted to fit in. I felt like I had been deprived of a lifetime of my own masculinity, and I wanted to make up for lost time. I wanted in on the world of men, but I wasn't sure how to gain access to it. I couldn't just demand it. I couldn't just slide in and pretend I had always been there. So I went searching for the spaces where I could be around other men, even if only in a book or a film.

It was easiest to find men's-only spaces in books about the military. I'd always been fascinated with the idea of war. I grew up reading the young-adult historical novel about the Revolutionary War *My Brother Sam Is Dead* and wondering what it would be like to be pressed into service. At night, as a child, I would tell myself stories to fall asleep. I would imagine I was a soldier in the army, ready to fight and kill in order to save my buddies. I was fascinated with my grandfather's stories of being in the US Navy. I played army with my best friend, Chris, as we ran through the woods pretending to be soldiers. I remember the anxiety of the first Gulf War, of not understanding what was happening but being caught up in a patriotic fervor (that was tinged with fear that our country would be under attack, and we'd be living through war on our own soil). In the stories I was seeing, it was all men. Men who joined the armed forces. Men who went off to defend their countries. Men who died. Even amid the fights for women to be allowed to enlist in combat roles and be taken seriously, I still mostly saw the military as a men's endeavor. So it makes sense that when I thought about men's-only spaces, I thought about combat units.

I've already shared my obsession with television shows and movies about war, even going as far as eating MREs and dressing in military clothing. In the midst of this, a friend asked me if I could only understand masculinity by being a part of violence. With everything I was seeing and experiencing in the world, it seemed like the answer was yes. That to be a man was somehow inextricably tied to violence: inflicting it or being the victim of it. But also the intimacy that I was hungry for seemed to be brought out by going through periods of trial together. I looked around at my classmates and just didn't see this same level of connection. Maybe they had it in ways I couldn't yet access, but it seemed they were doing their own jockeying for position and power. In the world of academia (and leftist academia), it was about whose thoughts were the most refined and purest. We didn't talk about our bodies. We didn't talk about our desires. We didn't talk about the loneliness that kept us up at night, wondering if we were good enough, if we were tough enough, if we were man enough.

My friends started to look at me funny. So did my wife, but I was trying to figure out something. What does it look like to be a man in this world? How do I understand my masculinity? Deeper than that, how do I find community with other men? What does it look like to be accepted into the ranks of men?

Lots of boys go through this phase, trying on identities, discarding the ones that don't fit. The problem for me was I was in my twenties. I was supposed to have this stuff figured out. I wasn't a child playing dress-up; I was a grown up. My experimentation was public and brought embarrassment. I think it's this fear of embarrassment that keeps a lot of us from trying on new ways of being, especially when the cost of being embarrassed is so high. We are not a culture that makes space for trying and failing. We're not a culture that makes space for figuring out your identity publicly, nor changing it once you've found it. Once a jock, always a jock. Once a nerd, always a nerd. And here I was, in my late twenties, dressed up like a soldier. No wonder people didn't know what to do with me.

In the beginning of my transition, I was hyper fixated on my appearance. I was taking testosterone to shape my body into the shape it should have been in, and I was desperate to recognize myself in the mirror. Every new hair, every crack in my voice, every shift in my body fat was cause for celebration. I took photos every month: from the front, the side, the back. Comparing them with the photos of the month before, looking and looking for the slightest change. Even as I was fixated, I was also uncomfortable.

When I started my transition, I was surrounded by men, but I didn't really feel like I was part of their community. It was like I wasn't quite sure how to fit in. Partly I wasn't sure that they saw me as one of their own yet. I remember distinctly the first time one of my friends used male pronouns for me and then followed up by acknowledging that it was the first time they were able to do that without thinking about it. It was both a beautiful moment and a little bit heartbreaking. I realized how othered I felt, even by people who conceptually really got it and wanted to accept me, who wanted to affirm me, but they still saw me as something not quite like who I really was. And so I didn't reach out to my male friends. I didn't ask them the questions that were burning inside me.

Instead, I went to forums, and online, I spent time with other transmasculine people. I searched all of the message boards and threads on LiveJournal, trying to figure out what other people's experiences were of navigating the world as a man. I've already mentioned that there were a couple of memoirs by transgender men, but they were pretty dated by the time I was coming out, written in the 1970s or '80s or '90s. And here it was, 2008. We were living in a different world. Already the upending of gender roles and gender norms was beginning. The medical community was starting to catch up to the fact that transgender men could look like all sorts of things. We weren't necessarily straight. Some of us were gay or bisexual. Some of us didn't want to sink into the world of masculinity without questioning what that really meant. And yet the memoirs that had been released were often from men who did want to slide into masculinity and seemed to not question very much about it.

With all the women I was surrounded by, with my relationships with women whom I loved and respected, women I looked up to, women whom I wanted to stay in community with, I needed to figure out a healthy way to be a man. I didn't want to be one of those guys who harassed women, or who made them feel unsafe, or who made them feel anything less than equal. But there were people from my own community telling me that somehow my transition was going to automatically make me into one of those guys. I wasn't quite sure what to do with that. And it is true that when I started taking testosterone, things shifted in my body: my sex drive went up, I did start to notice things more visually, my temper was quicker. And yet I didn't suddenly become some hormone-crazed maniac who was quick to violence. I was able to control myself. I didn't have to give in to any of the urges I might be feeling. That was a relief.

It seemed, though, that no matter where I looked, whether in the narratives of trans men or the narratives of men in the media, there was one common theme: Men were tough. They were ready to do violence if they or someone they loved were threatened. To be a man meant being hard. It also meant seeing everything as a competition. You needed to always be on the top of the heap, no matter what the situation. We were all in a competition, and the toughest person would win.

Certainly some men cried, and some men were tender, but the role of a man in the world was to be a tough guy. Protective. In charge. Not a pushover.

Whether it was people talking about raising boys ("They're so rough and tumble! Always getting into scrapes!") or training boys for sports or the military ("Toughen up! Be strong! Gut it out!"), there was a narrative that masculinity equaled toughness.

I've met a lot of trans guys who go through a hypermasculine phase. I went through one myself. Early in transition, when we're still probably not being seen as male very often, we try out different ways of being. If I act this way, does it feel better in my body? How about this way? If I speak like this, will people be more likely to read me as male? How about if I do this?

We're making up for a lifetime of being in a body that hasn't felt like ours, being in spaces where we don't feel like we fit. We're trying to make up for the boyhood we feel we've been robbed of. We might swagger a little more, walk with exaggeration, make jokes to set ourselves apart.

We're trying to fit in with the other guys, to be just like them, even if we don't particularly like how they behave. Sometimes this is also a coping mechanism: if we're in a place, being seen as male, and people are making jokes that make us uncomfortable, it can seem safer to stay silent or even laugh at the joke than it does to call someone out.

Most of us seem to outgrow this phase pretty quickly. We realize that we've traded one performance for another and try to find the posture that doesn't feel like acting. We realize we don't need to disparage or denigrate women in order to feel more masculine.

But we see this narrative still today, even as social mores have shifted. There is a sense in some corners of the world that the reason men are struggling is because they've lost their ability to be tough. Men have become soft. They are weak. In order to save men, we need them to get back to the ideal of toughness.

*　*　*

Every time I post about masculinity on social media, someone comes into my mentions to tell me that I should be looking up to Andrew Tate. He has become the new image bearer of the "ideal" masculinity. I have to admit, the first few times people mentioned his name to me, I didn't know who he was—beyond his arrest for sexual assault and trafficking, which I'd seen in the news. Because of that, I already knew I wasn't interested in his version of masculinity. A quick scan of his Wikipedia page confirmed my concerns: a history and pattern of sexism, misogynistic views, violence against women, and more. It's a litany of mess.

And yet there is something about him that appeals to other young men. Why? What is it about Tate's messaging that is appealing to anyone, and who, exactly, is it appealing to?

Tate is a former boxer who had a stint on *Big Brother* (he got removed after six days because a video of him being violent to a woman surfaced), and that started his fame—though it seems like TikTok did the rest. He sells online courses. He poses with lots of expensive cars and flaunts his wealth. He gleefully claims his sexism and his desire to date 18–19-year-olds.

The fact that Tate is lauded by young men is alarming to me. As a man, as someone who cares about young people, as someone who wants to believe in change, as someone who wants to believe the world is getting better, the fact that someone like Tate is being held up as an example for emulation is beyond concerning.

I have to admit I don't even want to consider why people are drawn to him. I don't want to do the work to say why his message resonates because I believe the message to be so toxic. And yet if he's being held up as the barometer of masculinity, it seems like, in a book about masculinity, not dealing with Tate would be an oversight.

There's a part of me that says Tate appeals to the immature. The boys who still aren't fully formed. Who are attracted by the idea of boxing and violence, access to women, and fast cars. But that doesn't feel like enough. Or it feels like letting both Tate and those boys off the hook.

There is something in Tate (and therefore in the wish fulfillment of his followers) that is about violence, power, wealth, and dominance. He is the myth of the tough guy writ large. The ideal that says if you're tough enough, you'll get all of these bonuses as well.

The easy thing is to say these are people who have felt disenfranchised, and they cling to anyone who makes them feel as if they could reclaim the power they feel entitled to. Do you see how often everything comes back to entitlement? Entitlement might be the number-one thing men have to deal with and overcome.

The thing with Tate and his followers is that in order for them to feel powerful, someone else has to be a victim. They're not satisfied with equality. In order for them to feel like they are men, they need to be over and above someone else. It's not about specificity of identity; it's not about equal but different—it's about power and being above.

These young men who flock to Tate don't feel connected. They don't feel like they have a place in the world. They don't feel like they have power and agency. They want someone to tell them what to do, tell them who to be. They want to believe in idols, believe in role models who can provide them with a sense of security.

And they also want flashy cars, cigars, dramatic wealth, and easy sex. My guess? They feel like none of those things are actually accessible to them, and instead of figuring out the real reasons why, they look to Tate to tell them that if they just follow his rules, they'll have everything they could ever want.

It's not surprising to me that Tate preys on young women— young women who feel like they have less power and agency, young women who are still being taught by everyone around them that they need to follow the rules to be accepted, young women who are being taught that the attentions of men are what they should be seeking above all.

When I tried to put on the persona of the tough guy, it didn't make me feel less afraid. In fact, it put me in greater danger. In my bravado, I was more willing to step up to someone and escalate a situation than try to de-escalate. I felt like I needed to be ready to jump into the fray instead of walking away. I was made to feel like my only tool was toughness or violence, and so I tried to make myself stronger.

The narratives of what made a man a "real man" were also centered on this idea of toughness. Real men were tested. They had proven themselves. So where did that leave those of us who hadn't been in battle or taken a punch? We walked around feeling like we didn't quite measure up. If we were gentle or kind, we were at risk of being considered less than.

We believe if I can just be tough enough, everything else will work itself out. No one will threaten me or the people I love. No one will make me feel less than. No one will make me feel afraid or alone or vulnerable.

But one of the narratives that gets overlooked when it comes to violence is how often men are a danger to ourselves and other men. According to the World Health Organization, "Men are overwhelmingly more likely than women to be both perpetrators and victims of interpersonal violence. In 2012, over half a million individuals worldwide died as a result of injuries from interpersonal violence. Of these deaths, males were disproportionately impacted: 81% of interpersonal violence deaths were men. In addition to being more likely to die as a result of violence, men, as a group, perpetrate more physical violence than women and perpetrate more harmful types of physical violence than women."

The myth of toughness makes us escalate situations that would be better served by calm and quiet. It forces us to put on a persona instead of expressing a full range of emotions. It asks us to keep people at arm's length because that's the only way the myth persists.

When we tell boys the only way to be men is through toughness, we push them into a box. We ask them to ignore their intuition and the range of feelings they might be experiencing. We plant seeds of inadequacy. We plant the question: what if I'm not tough enough to be a real man?

How do we unlearn the myth of toughness? First, by being present to the pressure it creates in our lives. Pay attention to when the urge to be tough causes you to repress another feeling or when it's not making you feel like you're being your best self. When is the idea of toughness making you feel like you're acting instead of coming home to who you truly are?

This isn't saying there's never a time or place to be tough. Sometimes we choose toughness in order to persist in achieving a goal. Sometimes we choose toughness in the pursuit of a cause that means a lot to us or when we're standing up for justice. There are times when toughness is necessary.

But toughness as the sole or best measure for masculinity isn't working for us anymore. Simply pushing through our pain, our grief, our exhaustion isn't helping us show up in the ways we want to show up. Being tough isn't all it's cracked up to be.

We need to refuse the idea that being tough is the only way of showing strength. There is strength in gentleness. There is strength in de-escalation. There is strength in knowing when to be tender and vulnerable.

CHAPTER SEVEN

Collaboration over Competition

I've always been a little competitive. Playing board games with my family growing up often ended in arguments and tears because my stepfather was even more competitive than I was. No one was allowing anyone else to win in our household. I remember one game of LIFE where I ended up flipping the board and storming out of the room when I felt the game wasn't going my way. I look back on it with embarrassment now, but I was only nine at the time and still didn't know how to moderate my emotions.

Competition isn't just about sports or board games, though. There seems to be competition everywhere. Between genders and religions and races. Between people who have money and those who don't. Between younger people and older people. We're taught to approach these competitions as zero-sum games: one group will win, and the other will lose. This is why there is often so much anxiety when one group starts to make progress: when they get some more protections under the law, when they gain access to areas and opportunities they had previously been denied access to, when they are seen and heard from more often.

Many men equate masculinity with power. To be masculine is to rule over other people. To be manly is to be tough, to be ready to throw a punch, to not let anyone speak to you in a way that feels disrespectful (whether it actually is or is just perceived). To be masculine is to walk into a room with a swagger and let everyone know who's boss. It's to rely on your masculinity to make you feel like you're powerful.

To men who believe this, anything that feels like weakness is to be shunned (whether in themselves or others). If they feel an emotion, if they feel tenderness, if they feel fear or shame, they push it away. They cover it over with anger and violence. They shore up their sense of themselves by doing harm to someone else, by putting them in their place, by making someone else feel small or weak so they don't have to.

But what happens when the ability to be big and strong stops working? What happens when your body doesn't respond in the way it used to? When you can't take a punch anymore? When you can't get your penis hard? When people don't back down in the face of your anger anymore? Do you just keep going after people you consider weaker and weaker? Do you push your body to listen to your commands? Do you find other ways to act out your rage (maybe with a gun)? Do you turn your rage on yourself?

In so many books about the crisis facing men and masculinity, it's framed in this competitive sense. Women are winning now, and so therefore men are losing. Women are gaining; men are falling behind. Instead of seeing this as a situation where the world is changing and we all need to be adapting and changing with it, it gets framed as winner take all. If the world is good for women, it will be bad for men. If the world is good for people of color, it will be bad for white people. If the world is good for LGBTQ+ people, it will be bad for heterosexual and cisgender people. These things are only true if your only definition of good equals dominating another group. If the only way men can be good is if they are in charge and in power, then yes, women progressing is going to feel like a threat.

So some men, feeling like they can't compete with women, turn instead to competing with other men. They try to be the strongest in the room. They fight to be the leader of the pack, the alpha, and to shame any man they consider weaker than them.

* * *

Into this fray step people like Jordan B. Peterson. Peterson is a psychologist who takes seriously the feeling of disorientation many young men experience. Peterson comes across as an intellectual. His book *12 Rules for Life: An Antidote to Chaos* promises a solution to the sense of floundering many young men feel. There are actually some things to applaud in

Peterson's rules. He encourages young people to find some discipline, to work on self-improvement, to look for ways to contribute. He encourages young men to surround themselves with people who will challenge them to be better and to choose to do hard things.

But underneath this good advice is Peterson's view that the world is about power and hierarchy and that men should be at the top of the hierarchy: "Walk tall and gaze forthrightly ahead. Dare to be dangerous. Encourage the serotonin to flow plentifully through the neural pathways desperate for its calming influence." In an online video, he tells men, "You should be a monster, an absolute monster, and then you learn how to control it." This idea that monstrosity is our birthright, our core way of being, and we need to feel it (even if we also need to temper it) focuses men on violence and competition.

In a world of gray, in a world that feels more confusing every single day, in a world where the old rules no longer apply, in a world where there is ambiguity, the Peterson rulebook is appealing. If you just do these twelve things, you'll be successful. If you do these twelve things, you'll have a place in the world. If you do these twelve things, you'll get what you want. It's the same appeal as fundamentalism: follow the rules, and you'll be good to go. You know instantly who's in and who's out. It's clear who belongs and who doesn't. It's clear who's part of our team and who isn't.

Rules are easy. If you know the rules, you know where you stand.

The rules of gender often feel similar: If you act like you're strong and tough, people will leave you alone. If you keep your eyes down in the bathroom, no one will bother you. If you pay for the date and open the door, people will want to go on a second date with you. If you look people in the eye and shake their hand firmly, you'll be respected. If you follow these rules, you'll be at the top of the hierarchy. You'll be the alpha. You'll get respect from everyone weaker than you, including other men.

*　*　*

The common narrative in popular culture echoes Peterson: Women want men to lead. It's good for men to be outspoken and bold. Speak your mind and don't hold back, and you'll be respected for it. Show that you can lead and be in charge. Men should be strong. Men shouldn't cry. Men should provide for their families (and, alternately, women should provide care for the household). Men should want to work with their hands.

Many of us grow up with these mantras taught to us. Some of us learn faster than others that many of these rules aren't true (or at least aren't true for us).

Still others are finding out that these mantras, if they were ever true, aren't true anymore. We're struggling to figure out how to exist in a world where the things we were taught as rules are actually holding us back now. It's no longer just that the rules don't apply but also that when we follow the rules, we seem to be punished for it. If we speak up and lead, we're told that we're taking up too much space. If we try to provide for our family, we're told we're buying into outdated notions of gender and robbing our partners of autonomy. If we are strong and we don't cry, we're told that we're repressed and unreachable emotionally.

But we also feel like we can't totally throw out the rules because if we cry all the time, people call us weak (or worse). If we expect our partners to split everything 50/50, we're still considered to be not doing our share. If we don't speak up in the meeting, then we're told that we're leaving everyone else to do all the work. It feels like we cannot win. Like whatever we do, we're doing it wrong.

Instead of questioning the rules (and if they ever should have been true in the first place), we begin to lash out at the people we feel are making it difficult for us. We lash out because we don't want to deal with having our equilibrium upended.

What feels much more complicated is empathy, compassion, and situational awareness. The idea that an action that is completely appropriate in one situation would be completely inappropriate in another is alarming. It's easier to blame changing mores than it is to grapple with our fault in the midst of it. So we look to new people who are willing to give us new rules. If you just believe these things, if you do these things, then you'll be good to go.

Having rules to follow means you never have to worry about whether or not you measure up. Having rules to follow means you never have to compare yourself with anyone else. You simply follow the rules.

So what if the rules keep changing, or if following them doesn't totally answer all the questions you have? Don't worry about that. Just keep on with the rules. What if other people don't like your rules? Well, then they're wrong, and you have a common enemy to unite against.

Jordan Peterson makes it easy for men to follow him because you never have to wonder. You never have to ask questions. You never have to think for yourself. You just do what he tells you, and you get to call yourself a successful man.

Since many of us were raised on competition—playing sports, trying to be the best in our class, coming out on top in every experience—it's no wonder that approaching life as a game with clear rules and even clearer winners and losers appeals to many of us. It makes us feel we have a sense of clarity about how to move through the world, a sense of control over how to get ahead.

But competition is no longer working. It's tearing us apart. It makes us see other people as opponents or, worse, enemies. We need to change our approach.

What if we looked at progress as separate from competition? What if we could understand there are no winners and losers? If we could do this, then we wouldn't be threatened when a group we don't belong to gets more access. It's not a zero-sum game. When it comes to living out the fullness of our humanity, we can all win. One group can't be fully human at the expense of another group. If one group is experiencing dehumanization, then they are experiencing it in the hands of another, thereby rendering the fullness of the humanity of the perpetrators null and void. In other words, unless we all win, none of us wins. Which means men can stop griping about women making advances. Straight people can stop worrying about queer folks getting more rights. Cisgender folks can stop demonizing transgender people for wanting to exist in public and do things like play sports and go to the bathroom. White people can stop worrying that people who are not white are taking away opportunities. We have to approach any issue that's confronting a particular group as one that inevitably impacts all groups.

At the same time, as we confront the places where men are falling behind, we need to look at both our own culpability and the actual systems that are at fault. We can say both that there are areas where men need to step up and be better and that there are systems that are failing us. As we look at issues facing men and boys in education and employment, it's clear that late-stage capitalism is causing a lot of harm to men. Yet it seems harder to critique that system because it's so ubiquitous. It's easier to blame other forces. So we blame the things befalling our masculinity on other groups of people. But we cannot look at loneliness, or marriage dissatisfaction, or lack of sex, or unemployment and blame women or queer or trans folks. And even as we look at systems like capitalism, we also have to face, head on, how we have fed into and continue to enforce systems of unhealth all by ourselves. In many ways, we have gotten ourselves into this mess, and we will have to get ourselves out of it.

We also cannot do it alone. This isn't a "pull yourself up by your own bootstraps" moment. While there is (and will continue to be) inner work for each of us to do, we also have to do this in community. We have to change how we interact with other men; we have to change how we interact with people of other genders. We need to do this not only to support one another but also to change the systems that keep us falling back into old patterns that hurt us and everyone around us. This is vulnerable work, and it will require us to be in community and move away from isolation. That's the only way this work will be sustainable for the long term.

* * *

These conversations about competition are complex and have a lot of layers, especially for gay and transgender men, but this is the work we need to be engaged in to both be healthy men and be good to the people of all genders surrounding us.

To unlearn competition, we first need to have a vision of mutual flourishing. What does a world look like where we all have what we need? What does it mean to be in cooperation with, instead of competition with, people? How do we participate instead of simply trying to win?

How can we come to terms with progress without feeling like we're losing out? How do we shift our mindset from one of scarcity to one of abundance? How do we celebrate the gains of groups we don't belong to while also focusing on how we might need to adapt in order to fit into a changing world?

Change is going to continue, and it's up to us to learn how to change with it. What does it look like to be a man when the things that we assumed we were going to get aren't just handed to us? (We'll talk more about this in a later chapter.)

Moving past ideas of competition to cooperation is going to take work. It will feel risky and vulnerable. We might feel exposed or weak, at least at first. But learning to cooperate, to be in community, to let our guard down will actually make us stronger in the long run. It will deepen our connections to people of all genders, it will make us more resilient, and it will allow us to work together to find creative solutions to the issues facing our world today.

CHAPTER EIGHT

Femininity Is Not the Enemy

Navigating masculine spaces can sometimes feel fraught. I want to interrupt bad behavior when it's happening in my presence. I want to be someone who de-escalates hostile situations. I want to be a model of how to treat people with respect and how to honor differences. I want to be in solidarity with every other marginalized group. And I am also sometimes afraid. Afraid of the violence of other men, afraid of my own lack of strength, afraid to be outed and then assaulted. I speak up as often as I can, but there have been times when I remained silent for fear of my own safety.

One night, my car got towed for some infraction I'm still not clear on. The bus route doesn't go to the impound lot, and so I had to wait until a friend got off work to take me there. I arrived with my information and my payment and was told to go stand in a line. A little later, a driver pulled up in a minivan, and I and a couple of other people got into the vehicle. The Minneapolis impound lot is massive, covering acres and acres of land, and filled with wrecks and parts—and somewhere in all of that mess was my car. The procedure is that the driver takes you through the lot to your car, then you drive it out, show your paperwork, and head on home.

By this point, it was dark out, and I was in a vehicle with two other guys and a woman. She got to her car first, and now it was just me and the two other guys. One had clearly been drinking. And now that it was just us guys in the car, they started to say offensive things about women. I was several years into my transition at this point but still learning confidence. I hated the stuff they were saying. I wanted to call them out on it. But I looked out the window and saw that I was in the middle of this massive lot, in the dark, with two men who were much bigger than me. I stayed silent and hoped that I would get to my car as quickly as possible.

On the way home that night, I felt terrible. I felt like I violated my own morals and ethics. And yet I also felt very aware of my fragility in that vehicle. I was worried that if I said something, something about the way I said it would out me as trans, and then I would be at the mercy of those two men.

I don't want to be afraid of other men, but I often am. I fear their anger. I fear their violence. I have seen men turn on a dime, joking and laughing one second to throwing a punch the next. I have seen men refuse to be de-escalated, as if backing down somehow makes them weak, even as they prove their weakness by refusing to listen to reason. I fear the way men use sexuality as a weapon, how they will threaten to rape or assault anyone who doesn't show them the right deference, and how they don't even think about what that says about them.

I am a man, and yet I am afraid of other men. I have this feeling I am not alone in that. Not just among other trans men but among cisgender men as well. After all, the statistics show that "regardless of the victims' sex, a greater percentage of violent incidents involved male offenders (79%)." Men are a threat, and if you're going to face violence, statistically the person doing it is more likely to be male. We have seen the damage men have wrought, and we are afraid of it. Herein lies the rub; by backing down in those moments, we allow the behavior we are afraid of to continue. The men who choose violence, who refuse to de-escalate, who wield their penises like weapons, who turn to shame and abuse in order to have power—they rely on no one standing up to them. They rely on their might in order to stay at the top. And because of the ways they have shored up their identity with violence, they are able to push back those of us who are (rightly) afraid of their wrath. When we refuse to stand up to them because we are afraid of being their victims, we open the door for them to hurt people even less equipped than we are to push back.

This is how hierarchies stay firmly in place; those closest to the power don't call it out because they are afraid of being treated like those without the power. I feel like I should have said something in that minivan. I should have told those guys to shut up. I should have made it very clear that everything they were saying was unacceptable, and I was a man who was not going to allow it in my presence. At the very least, I should have reported the driver to his superiors after the fact. But I was afraid, and so their behavior went uncommented on, which cemented in their minds that this type of behavior was acceptable, it was agreed on by other men, and it was something that allowed them to feel more powerful.

This experience is familiar to every single woman. They've all had moments of clutching their keys as they walk to their cars at night, of being in elevators with men who were creepy, of feeling their hearts race when they hear footsteps behind them at night. I, too, have felt those feelings. I've walked with my keys clutched in my fist. I've checked under my car before getting in. I've been socialized and trained in these methods of survival. I feel like I still need them.

It's a complex balance because I also realize that in many situations, I'm the man who might make a woman uncomfortable. I do my best to stay far away from women when walking on the street, especially at night. I'll often cross to the other side when no one else is around so they know I am not following them. I'll verbally tell someone I'm passing when I come up too fast behind.

Many men seem to feed off of this energy or at least not question it. Certainly most of us don't want to cause women to be afraid, but we think nothing of making disparaging remarks about women when we're out with our friends ("Women . . . am I right?") or considering ourselves as completely separate from women and their reality. We have so internalized misogyny that we often don't even question it. The amount of hatred, loathing, and disgust I've seen and heard from men (including gay and bisexual men) often astounds me.

Early in my transition, I was hanging out with Amy (my partner at the time), and I made a joke that I had made a thousand times before. It was a well-worn one between Amy and me, but this time she bristled. I didn't understand. I wasn't sure what was different, but something clearly was. I had done something wrong without even realizing it. I replayed the conversation in my mind. The joke. Her response. It didn't make sense. We'd had this same interaction a million times in situations just like this. What was different?

It took me longer than it should have to realize: *I* was different. On testosterone. Identifying as male. Sometimes being seen as male. The joke I made, once funny between two women, held an entirely different tenor now that I was no longer a woman.

At the time, I was frustrated. Why couldn't she see that I was the same? Our relationship was the same. Nothing had to change just because I was on T because I was, after all, the same person she fell in love with. The same person she married. On the one hand, that is categorically true. I am still me. I am Shannon, just as I have always been Shannon. But now with some years' distance and a lot more understanding of power and oppression and privilege, I realized that my desire for our relationship to stay the same was based on naivety. Because of the way the world is structured, our relationship couldn't stay the same. Even as I was the same person, our dynamic was different because people saw me differently. I wasn't able to hide behind the idea that I was the same person as before when the entire world was structured to see and treat me differently.

Part of my journey of masculinity has been learning to navigate these spaces and situations. But because there are so few models, I've often been on my own. Some people would say that I shouldn't have backed down; I should have said what I wanted to say and told my partner to not be so sensitive. Others would have said that me shifting my behavior meant I wasn't very manly or that I was capitulating when I didn't have to. But I think the power of having to define and learn masculinity for myself is the power to shift and change and grow. I can look at that situation, realize the power dynamics had changed, and change myself so that I could be leading toward equality.

Having to be on my own gender journey has made me very aware of the choices we have when we are in spaces and how many men choose to ignore those choices in order to default to whatever makes them the most comfortable. By the same token, because I am, in some ways, outside of masculinity due to how I was raised and socialized, I can sit in a room and see the power move through it. I can see how everyone is weaving in and out of gendered dynamics. I can see the people who are trying to subvert them and the people who aren't even trying. It's this fine dance between inhabiting my masculinity while also being aware of the ways in which I am wielding it and wearing it in order to do no harm.

Where is the moment when I can use my inherited power to move a situation toward justice and liberation? Where are the moments when the best way for me to be a good man is to shut up and get out of the way? Where are the moments when it's something in the middle? It's a complicated calculus and one that I am very aware of pretty much every moment of every day.

*   *   *

One of the critiques of transgender men from people who argue that transgender people shouldn't (or don't) exist comes from lesbian communities who say that trans men are self-hating women. Our transitions are misogyny because we are choosing to reject our own "femininity." They also claim that the rise of transgender men is relatively new and we are destroying the idea of being a tomboy, that trans men are forcing children into trans identities instead of letting kids be kids. These arguments ignore the fact that transgender men have existed for at least hundreds of years (and presumably longer but either didn't have the language or were written out of the historical record) and that many transgender men are very clear that we do not hate women or even femininity; we just aren't either of those things.

But these arguments underscore how fraught it is to talk about gender, especially when we live in systems where certain people are (and have been) oppressed because of their gender. What does it mean for someone to, at least with how it appears on the surface, leave an oppressed gender and join forces with the oppressor? That's the question these folks are asking—but it denies the reality of transgender men's lives and transitions. We are not leaving womanhood; we were never actually a part of it even if we were assumed to be a part of it. At the same time, we did live and move in those spaces, and so we often know what it was like to be treated as a woman. We experienced, firsthand, the dismissal of our ideas, the fetishization of our bodies, the abuse and harassment. We experienced the lower pay and the struggle to access the things we need.

Yet even as we transition to becoming ourselves, we often don't have full access to the privileges of masculinity. Transgender people struggle to find employment and are often un- or underemployed. Transgender people struggle to find stable housing, as well as adequate health insurance and medical care, and are often victims of abuse. While the numbers are clearly worse for transgender women (particularly transgender women of color), transgender men face significantly worse outcomes than their cisgender counterparts. Add on compounding marginalizations such as transgender men of color, trans men who are gay or bisexual, trans men with disabilities or who are neurodivergent, and you'll see other harrowing statistics. We don't have full access to cisgender male privilege, and yet we do have more privilege than transgender women. It's complicated. Transgender men have unique needs, and it's important that we don't overlook them even as we keep the focus on those who are most marginalized.

These nuances don't fit into pithy soundbites. They're not easily reduced to an infographic that can be shared on social media. They often bring up strong emotions in everyone involved, so a lot of people either don't talk about this at all or they do whatever they can to retreat back to conversations that are easier to digest (like the ones about trans men abandoning the cause of women and joining their oppressors). But if we're ever going to get free, we have to be willing to lean into the nuance. We can't reduce everything to its easiest quote. We have to understand all of the complexities.

There's an idea that's been gaining in popularity that I think is helpful to bring up here. It's called *whataboutism*. The idea is that in a conversation where one person is sharing their experience or talking about oppression, particularly on social media, someone will come into the comments and say "what about . . ." So if a transgender man talks about the violence and oppression he faces, someone will come into the comments and say, "What about trans women? Don't you know they have it so much worse?" And the answer is yes, we do know that trans women (especially trans women of color) fare worse on many, many fronts. But that doesn't erase the oppression that trans men face as well.

Sometimes whataboutism is used to distract from the actual issue at hand. If a women's justice organization talks about the need for women to be able to get divorced, sometimes men in the comments will "what about" their ability to have custody or visiting rights with their children. Both issues are important, but bringing up the one in the context of the other serves, often, to distract or derail the conversation.

We need to be able to talk about all of it. The way men have continually harmed women and benefited from patriarchy *and* the ways that men's mental health is more dire than ever.

There is often a subtle (and sometimes not so subtle) hatred of the feminine and women laced through masculinity. Many men have been taught that women are less than men—they are less strong, less capable, less important—and whether we believe that or not, it creeps into how we think about and talk about women.

Many cisgender men feel justified in making offensive jokes when they are in men's-only spaces. They see nothing wrong with saying something incredibly crass and then going home to their wife or their girlfriend and being sweet and kind. There is a casual misogyny that gets excused when men get together, as "boys will be boys."

We see this play out during gender reveals when men are disappointed to find out that their new child is presumed female. (There have been a couple of videos that have gone viral, but it's popular enough that there's an entire search section for the phrase *man gets angry at gender reveal* that turns up a lot of results.) We see it in the ways that men accuse other men of being effeminate as a way to shame them and denigrate them. We use feminized terms as insults without thinking twice. We have internalized the hatred of women to such a degree that it's normalized.

This misogyny isn't just among straight men. The amount of anti-woman conversations I've heard in gay men's spaces is a lot. Often, gay men speak about women's bodies as if they are disgusting. They see their lack of attraction to women as justification for calling their bodies vile and gross. It often goes unmentioned, or when it is called out, it gets played off as a joke.

Transgender men are not immune to misogyny, both internalized and acted out. It feels important to note that sometimes what appears like misogyny in trans men is actually an incredibly deep self-loathing for all that feels feminine in ourselves. It's often a complex intersection of internalized mores, self-hatred/loathing, and trying to figure out how to fit into society, especially a society that often seems to not want us. This doesn't excuse bad behavior, but it does illustrate how incredibly complex these feelings are. It's not that we hate women or think they aren't equal to us; it's that we hate being *seen* as women. Not because women are bad but because we aren't them. It's easy to cross the line, though, from hating ourselves to acting out that hatred on other people. It's why this inner work is so vital. We have to make sure that as we're working out our own feelings and masculinity, we're not doing harm to people we want to be in relationship and solidarity with.

Sometimes trans men participate in casual misogyny because of fears about safety. The moment you laugh at a joke in a bar or don't call someone out for saying something offensive. The moment you might say, "Women . . . am I right?" in order to fit in. It's not right; it's something we need to work on, too, but it's also often a way of navigating spaces that might suddenly become hostile if we're not careful. The thing is that many cisgender men do the same and sometimes even for the same reasons, but with trans men, we're more attuned to the moods of the people around us. We can read the room, and we understand exactly what games everyone is playing. We have learned how to keep ourselves safe, and that safety relies on always knowing our surroundings.

For many of these reasons, I went through a hypermasculine phase early in my transition. I was trying to make sure people could actually see me, that they could see the man I was becoming. And since I still didn't always look like the man I was becoming, I tried to show it through my mannerisms. By trying to walk differently, by lowering my voice, by becoming obsessed with the military and men's-only spaces. I was uncomfortable with the feminine in me and wanted to excise it.

Later, when I was seen properly most of the time, I felt less of a need to put on manners that felt hypermasculine. I could settle into my natural register of masculinity because the visual cues were now enough for people to gender me appropriately. That all took time. And it was confusing because I didn't have the self-awareness at the time to really articulate what I was going through. I just knew I had this drive to be seen as who I knew myself to be.

For other transgender men, it's a desire to distance themselves from the feminine. Partly because they were forced into those spaces for so long, partly to gain entry into the masculine spaces they long to be in, partly to figure out what it means for them to be a man (and feeling they can't do that while they are still too intertwined with femininity). The problem in all of this is that on the outside, it simply looks like everyone else's misogyny. It functions the same way, it hurts in the same way, and it's why we need to talk about all of this with some nuance. Because even though these behaviors from trans men might be understandable, even forgivable, they are still part of a toxic system of masculinity that denigrates women and the feminine. It also highlights how strong the power of the patriarchy is that even people who were brought up being (inaccurately) considered women, being socialized and raised that way, still internalize negative messages about women and femininity. It shows how important this deep unlearning work is and how hard it is.

While many cisgender men don't fear violence, though some surely do, they also have internalized the ways to keep the men around them happy. They, too, know how to read a room and try to prevent violence. They might not entirely understand what it is they're doing, though, or how they are helping uphold the very system that makes them feel unsafe. Most transgender men are clearer about what it is they're doing because they've learned to be hyper attuned to the spaces they're in and the people around them. We've learned how to watch other men and mimic their behaviors so we fit in better. Since there are no manuals on how to be a man, we are forced to observe and document and try to make sense of all the unspoken rules around masculinity. Often, casual misogyny is a big part of this equation. We strike first so we won't be struck. We parrot the jokes in order to keep ourselves safe and keep anyone from questioning our identities.

So how do transgender men keep from perpetuating systems of harm while also being the people we are? One of the ways is to separate the personal from the systemic. While we realize that we are not women, we know that women exist and face unique challenges because of the way society is structured. We are not relinquishing our womanhood. We are not abandoning the fight. We are not transitioning because being a woman is too hard. We are transitioning to become ourselves. We can see ourselves as individuals who need to make a change in order to be more in alignment with who we are without needing to denigrate or dismiss the women other people assumed we were or the women we were once in community with.

Other trans men have talked about losing friends and losing a sense of community as they transition. They aren't sure how to fit in with the men around them (even as they are one), and yet they no longer feel welcome in the spaces they once called home. This sense of being in between, of not being sure where you fit, is one that many non-transgender men will have to face as we embark on the work to be better men. As we start raising questions, going deeper with the people around us, changing our behavior, and seeking to be more vulnerable, there will be people who turn away. We can't let that stop us from pursuing the healthy relationships we long for. There might be people with whom we grow distant or even cut ties. Not everyone will be willing or able to grow with us, to enter into these new spaces of vulnerability and risk. But does that mean it's not worth it to do the work? Not at all. In fact, we owe it to ourselves and the communities we come from to be the best possible versions of ourselves.

Next, we have to grapple with our hatred of women and our misogyny. Part of that work is understanding that women don't exist simply for our pleasure. They do not exist in opposition to us. Women are not what we are measuring ourselves against. These sound like simple statements, but I've met too many men who take these things for granted to feel like I can let them go unsaid. If women aren't our opposition or our opposites, if women aren't here for our pleasure or for us to dominate, then we can begin to see them as partners, not as something to avoid.

We need to get rid of the ideas that "men are from Mars and women are from Venus" or that we're two different species who will never understand each other. Instead, we need to understand that the health of people of all genders and identities is bound up together. We get free together. We can complement each other without being in competition. We can learn from one another. We don't have to be separate. In order to enter into equal relationships, we can't disparage each other. We can't denigrate women to make ourselves feel better. We can't revile their bodies. We can't deprive them of their own agency or see them as objects.

We have to deal with our own fears of being considered feminine and start to call out other men who use the feminine as a pejorative. Softness, kindness, gentleness, tenderness are things to be lauded, not put down. We need these things in ourselves and others. These aren't weak traits. These aren't traits to be banished. These are traits to be coveted and grown in us and our communities.

CHAPTER NINE

We Cannot Do This Alone

The men I grew up around didn't seem to have a lot of friends. They had buddies. Acquaintances. They had people they played sports with or went hunting with. They would talk to the husbands of their wife's friends, but when it came down to it, I didn't see the men in my life being deeply invested in relationships. Sometimes they were part of a men's-only small group or went on a men's retreat, but it wasn't the same as the women in my life. The women had friends, and they made time for those friends. When they were together, they talked deeply about what was going on in their lives and how they felt about it. The men, on the other hand, well, they seemed pretty lonely.

This loneliness in men isn't a new thing, though it seems to be getting worse. Reports have started to come out lately about the "friendship recession," how many people have fewer and fewer friendships. While it's affecting people of all genders, it's impacting men the most. For instance, "the percentage of men with at least six close friends fell by half since 1990, from 55 percent to 27 percent. The study also found the percentage of men without any close friends jumped from 3 percent to 15 percent, a fivefold increase. Single men fare the worst. One in five American men who are unmarried and not in a romantic relationship report not having any close friends."

When I think about the models of masculinity we've been handed, the idea of John Wayne looms large. Well, not actually John Wayne but the mythos he inspires. John Wayne has, in some ways, become not just a movie star but also an archetype in his own right. He's the symbol of the "masculine ideal" for a lot of folks. Strong and silent, ready to defend his people and his women. He'll fight you as soon as he'll look at you. He doesn't need to talk much, just a well-delivered one-liner before he shoots you dead.

Same with the Marlboro Man, another icon of masculinity. Perched atop his horse, smoking a cigarette. Riding off into the sunset *alone*. Maybe, every once in a while, sharing a silent can of beans over a fire with another silent man.

There is a lot that's problematic about these iconic figures— their connection with American myths of manifest destiny and the violent colonization of Indigenous people and lands, for one. Their connection with stereotypes of male toughness, anger, and violence, for another. But for the purposes of this chapter, it's most important to observe that when John Wayne and the Marlboro Man did anything, they did so *alone*. They didn't need anyone. In fact, they didn't *want* anyone.

The idea of the lone figure on a horse "settling new land" has never been a reality. It's always been a myth, part of the lie we've told ourselves about the United States and white people's role here. And yet the idea that men should go it alone, should be self-sufficient, should take what's "theirs" seems to refuse to die.

It leads to a sense of entitlement in men who subscribe to these ideals. It leads to a refusal to talk about, confront, or deal with emotions and feelings, wanting instead to shove them down and pretend they don't exist. Men shouldn't need anyone or anything, so they hold themselves apart from the people in their lives, even their spouses, children, and friends. Men are supposed to be stoic, which means they don't express joy or love or compassion. (Somehow stoicism as an idea allows men to be super angry without violating their "stoicness," even though in Stoic philosophy, being able to control your anger and rage is one of the main tenets.)

It seems silly to talk about men refusing to ask for directions or trying to fix things they have no business fixing as a sign of a masculinity that is out of sync with the world around it, but it's part of this idea that men don't need anyone or anything. It starts with directions and ends with men's refusal to go to the doctor or a therapist. It starts with men believing they don't need anyone and ends with men's significantly higher rates of suicide.

Our refusal to ask for help is literally killing us. From the health problems that could have been easily solved had they been caught early enough (and if we had actually taken our medication) to the mental health problems that spiral out of control because we believe we can solve them on our own. We need to shake off the myth of the Marlboro Man. We were never meant to be self-sufficient. Besides, self-sufficiency has always been a myth. We have always depended on other people to help us provide for ourselves. Even farmers who provided food for their families still purchased supplies at the store. They still purchased fabric for clothing. They still depended on their community to help them take in the harvest at the end of the season.

Asking for help isn't just about admitting you can't do it alone. It's about realizing you are part of a community. We do things for one another. We support each other. We give and accept help. This isn't a sign of weakness; it's a sign of friendship. It's a sign of community. And in a world where our loneliness is reaching epidemic levels, we need more community. We need to feel like we're a part of something. This sense of belonging isn't just good for our mental health; it's also good for our physical health: "Loneliness and social isolation are associated with a 29% increased risk of heart disease and a 32% increased risk of stroke in adults 50 and older. Social deficits are also linked to a higher likelihood of early death."

But in order to be a part of something, we have to contribute, and we have to be willing to receive as well. It's about being in relationship. It always has been. Yet we're often afraid to admit we need intimacy and relationships with other people, especially other men.

* * *

Our culture is pretty terrible about teaching us how to make friends. The ways we used to find, make, and keep friends are changing. In the past, many more people stayed near one place their entire life or at least their entire adult life. You stayed longer in jobs so had more of an opportunity to make friends with your coworkers. People joined more organizations—churches, the Lions Club, or the Kiwanis, for instance—and maintained relationships that way. Now people are more transient. We move more often. We leave jobs every couple of years. We don't join those organizations either because they feel outdated or because we know we won't be staying in one place for very long. So the old ways of making friends no longer exist for many of us, and yet we haven't replaced those old ways. We still expect to make friends at work or to stay in touch with our buddies from school even as we move to new cities and experience shifts in our thinking.

How many of us grew up seeing our fathers invested in deep friendships with other men? How many of us had modeled for us a man taking the reins of friendship in his life, especially friendship that wasn't tied to an activity? I remember my stepfather playing on the church softball team or going on hunting weekends with other guys (where they mostly sat alone in tree stands all day long). But simply going out with a friend to talk or having a friend over for dinner rarely happened unless my mother planned it and it was with another couple.

There's nothing wrong, per se, with friends based on activities. In fact, doing more things out in the world with other people would be good for a lot of guys. Get us out of the house and conversing with others. But when it's only activities, it robs us of the chance to have deeper conversations. There's only so much depth you can get into between screaming at your team on the television or between innings at the ball game.

Yet this is how we've been taught to make friends. Just do more stuff. And this is what we've been taught friendships between men entail. We do things together. We watch things together. There is always an event, an activity.

I'm an introvert. I will happily spend days without leaving the house or conversing verbally with anyone other than my partner. I cherish my alone time. I spend a lot of time in my head, thinking deeply, writing, reading, puzzling out answers to questions. I also moved to a completely new town and state about two years ago. With all of that, you'd think I wouldn't have very many friends or that making friends is hard for me, but even in my new community, I've already found friends with whom I share deep and heartfelt connections.

Yet over and over again, I hear from people that they struggle to make friends. They don't know how to connect with people.

I'm a part of a couple of online communities. One of the most common reasons people join these communities is because they are looking for friendships; they want to connect with other people. Yet time and time again, I am shocked at how little these folks interact with one another. They'll pop into the community and unload about something that's stressing them out but then not respond to a single one of the comforting comments people leave. Or they'll answer a discussion question but never respond to anyone else's answers. I'll talk to someone who feels lonely, and I'll ask if they've reached out to any of their friends. They say no, they don't want to have to be the one to reach out.

Many heterosexual cisgender men put this burden on their partners and wives. The women become the ones to set up the couple's date nights, they reach out to friends, they are the ones to keep track of birthdays and anniversaries, buying and sending the cards from both of you. They are the ones who keep up on who might need an extra hand, who's having health troubles or having a crisis. They reach out and connect, and the men come along for the ride. Maybe there's a monthly game night or a gathering to watch the Super Bowl, but even then, partners are preparing the food and making sure everyone has everything they need.

On an episode of Deep Questions with Cal Newport, Newport tackled the idea of the friendship recession and how so many men are lacking any kind of friends. He interviewed Jamie Kilstein about his work and quest to reboot his life and find and form deep male friendships. Jamie spoke about how one of the big hindrances he faced in his quest was his own indoctrination about "being considered too gay." He talked about his experience being that the last time he had a group of friends was in high school. Those friends would call each other *gay* for all sorts of things—for being too interested in something, for being too into their emotions, and for having an interest in being friends with another guy. He had to overcome these deep-seated fears he'd been carrying with him since high school, including the fear that if he wanted to have friendships with other men, he was somehow not masculine enough.

He also shared that as he was beginning his quest to have more male friends, part of his process was becoming interested in doing things. It was going out and getting involved in things and then paying attention to the guys he was drawn to, the ones who were also doing those things. These were guys who made him want to do more, be more, and improve himself. He talked about coming home from outings and gushing about these guys, in the same way that he would maybe gush about a girl he had a crush on. He said all of this with no judgment; this was part of the process. He was getting interested in other people, seeing what lit him up and whom he wanted to surround himself with.

What I was really struck by was both his acknowledgment that part of the thing that kept him from having more male friends was his fear of not being enough and how nervous he was about being the first person to reach out to another guy. He was nervous about asking them to do things; he was nervous they weren't going to like him or he wasn't going to be considered cool enough or they weren't going to be interested in his friendship. But the other half was that he had to overcome his own fears about being considered unmasculine.

That somehow desiring to be friends with other men, desiring deeper friendships and relationships, desiring intimacy, wanting to overcome his own loneliness was also about overcoming the programming that said wanting those things made him somehow unmasculine or unmanned. This is a key part in this epidemic of loneliness facing men. This is one of the things we have to talk about and overcome. What about our programming? What about the messages we internalized about what it means to be a man? Do we need to overcome something in those messages in order to be good friends or to be in better relationship with other people?

If we're going to have the deep friendships we're longing for, we have to take some responsibility for the relationships in our lives. We have to reach out to people (intentionally and not just when we have a problem). We have to ask questions about their lives. We have to keep track of important things like birthdays and anniversaries. I'm sure you're using a calendar. When you remember it's someone's birthday, put it in your calendar and set it to repeat every year. You'll never forget again. You can do this for other important things as well, like wedding anniversaries or the date when someone close to your friend died. Many of us seem to have this idea that women's brains are just better suited to remembering things when really it's that we don't care enough to figure out systems to remember. We offload our responsibility, once again, onto our partners, creating more mental load on them and letting ourselves off the hook. We have to stop doing this.

Forming friendships doesn't have to feel scary. It doesn't have to feel like a free fall into vulnerability (in fact, it probably shouldn't be). It simply needs to be done with intention. There's someone in your life who you like hanging out with. Every once in a while, send a text that says "Hey, was thinking about you. What's up?" Maybe the first couple of times they don't respond. Or they respond with something shallow. But you keep sending those texts, you keep expressing interest, you actually listen when they do share something and see how it shifts your relationship.

Following up with people also matters. If you're watching the game with a friend, and he mentions he's got a doctor's appointment coming up, or a job review, or an interview, in a couple of weeks, ask how it went. Check to make sure everything is okay. Little things like that go a long way.

It's okay to be the one to reach out. At first, you might be the only one reaching out. That doesn't mean people aren't interested, or the relationship is one-sided; they just might need to learn what it means to be a friend.

What if you're a guy who has at least some connections? You maybe have some work buddies or some relationships with other guys you do things with. Maybe you belong to a church or a civic organization. You don't feel completely lonely, but you also have a sense something is missing.

Maybe it's a longing for deeper connection. Maybe the group you're a part of subscribes to a form of masculinity you're beginning to find restrictive. Maybe you've been following all the unspoken rules of your group, and it's not giving you the life you want. Maybe you're starting to feel like the way these guys are telling you that you should behave is in conflict with what actually works best for the relationship you're in and the way your family life is structured. You're starting to feel a bit like a fish out of water, out of step with the people around you.

The problem with the way many of our groups are structured, especially groups around a common cause (like a religious belief system, the playing of a certain kind of sport, a shared past experience), is that often there is a flattening of experience. You are part of the group because you behave like this, believe like this, show up like this. The rightful fear, then, is if you start showing up differently, will you still be welcome? If you start to question the beliefs of your church, will you still be part of the group? If you start to call the guys out on their sexist jokes, will you still get invited to watch the game? If you start to show up in the space differently, will you still be included? These questions, which get to the desire for so many of us to "do it right" and to "be the right kind of man," keep many of us from asking any questions at all. We continue to try to contort ourselves into groups and relationships that no longer fit because we're worried the questions we're asking and the ideas we're exploring will cause people to judge us.

The reality is that they might. Certain groups are notorious for being closed communities. You are welcome as long as you show up the way they're asking you to and don't ask too many questions. These types of groups also keep us from making change because we want to belong. We don't want to be alone, or on the outside, or feel like we're not part of the community. So we shut up, and we show up, and things continue without changing.

You might worry that if you leave these groups, things will be even worse. Won't you join the throngs of men who are experiencing deep loneliness? But is it really friendship if you're only accepted because you follow all the rules? Is it really community if it can't withstand a difference of opinion? Are you really welcome if you have to change yourself in order to walk in the door?

To unlearn the myth of the solitary man, we first have to examine our own lives. What keeps us from reaching out to other men? Are we afraid of being rejected by them? Are we afraid that we won't measure up to their definitions of masculinity? Are we afraid we're unworthy or not enough? Are we afraid they'll think we're somehow unmasculine for wanting friends or they won't accept us because we're gay or trans?

Why do we only or mostly turn to women for emotional support and connection? Why are we afraid or anxious around other men? We need to sit with our answers to these questions. Too many of us rely on women for emotional support because we're afraid to be vulnerable with the men in our lives, but this leads to an increasing imbalance in our relationships and the inability of men to encourage one another toward healthier expressions of our masculinity. Men need male friendships. (We need friendships with people of other genders, too, but we also need friendships with men.)

Once we've identified what's holding us back, we begin to work through it by making small gestures. Remember that friendship takes time. It takes an investment of energy and attention. Loneliness might not be solved overnight, but you can also start right now to alleviate it.

If you don't know any men whom you might invite to go do something, think about what activities you might do where you might meet men. Maybe you're really into board games. Is there a local game shop where you can find some folks to play a game with? Can you join a local sports team? Can you take some kind of class at a community center? Getting out of your usual routine and putting yourself into a place where you can meet new people might be the first step to friendship.

If you already have some men in your life, are there people you know who won't reject you or make fun of you? Start with them.

Be the one to reach out and extend an invitation. Start to pay attention to what people say to you and remember it, then ask about it the next time you hang out. Remember important dates like birthdays and anniversaries. Host an event at your place or at a neutral place where you can actually have a conversation (meaning not a bar where you need to scream to be heard).

"Okay," I can hear you thinking. "I get that if I want things to change, I have to start showing up differently, but the reason I show up tough is because if I don't, I get treated badly. So what's the solution?" Many of us have figured out ways of being that allow us to blend in. We've learned that standing out puts us at risk. It makes us a target. So we strive to get through every interaction by flying under the radar. We're neither the most aggressive nor the quietest guy in the room. We're not the total asshole, but we're also not the pushover. We've crafted a perfect blend of bluster and kindness in order to make sure we're no one's target. I can understand feeling some nervousness about showing up differently. After all, if someone is heavily invested in a certain type of masculinity, they're probably not going to change just because we change. So how do we deal with that?

We do this by starting small. The eventual goal is to transform all of our interactions, but that doesn't mean we need to transform all of them at once. You don't need to show up to the next Super Bowl party and try to have everyone go deep into how their personal lives are going and how they're feeling about it (though you certainly could). Instead, think about the one guy in your life who you think is on a similar journey. One guy you think would be open to going a little deeper, shifting the conversation a bit, and showing up more fully.

It's important, in this moment, to reiterate that I'm asking you to find another man to have these conversations with.

So often when we decide we want to go deeper, we reach out to the women in our lives. We go to our wife or a female friend because we know they'll be receptive to talking about feelings. But the point of this work is to be able to have these conversations with other men. To learn how to be in community. It's not fair to always go to women and expect them to help us have hard or emotional conversations. We can't keep making them teach us how to be emotionally mature. We need to take responsibility for our own emotional development and for the emotional development of our friend groups. Which isn't to say don't show up with vulnerability with the women in your life. But if you're only showing up to talk about emotions with women, then you're still expecting them to do labor for you. You're treating them differently than the men in your life; you're expecting them to meet needs for you that you're not sure you can get met elsewhere. This is why we're in these situations. We have to learn how to talk to one another.

So think about that guy in your life who you believe would be open to all of this. Start with him. Start to open up a bit more. When he asks how things are going, don't just deflect; actually tell him. Ask him to tell you as well. If he deflects (and he might), ask again. Tell him you really want to know. You don't have to force it; if he deflects again, let it go (but ask again the next time you hang out). Remember, you're struggling to change, so he might struggle too. He might feel like you're trying to set him up or you don't really care, or he might not know how to answer. He might need to see you do it a couple of times before he feels his own confidence to return the vulnerability. It might take some time.

As you start to have more conversations with this one friend, pay attention to how it feels. It might feel weird at first or uncomfortable. It might feel like nothing is changing. Give it time.

You went on a date with your partner. Beyond what you did and what you talked about, how did it feel? What new thing did you learn about your partner? Was there anything in the interaction that felt difficult or like you didn't know what to do or say? How are you feeling about your partner? Do you feel close or distant? Are you having fun, or are you wanting more commitment? What is it like to be building a life with this person? Or if you're not there yet, can you picture building a life with this person?

You had a hard week at work. What happened? How is it making you feel? Are you frustrated? Burnt out? Feeling overlooked or taken advantage of? Are you struggling to make sense of a new employee? Are you wondering if you might want to start looking for another job? What does that thought bring up in you?

You might be thinking this sounds silly or like I'm telling you how to make friends or have a conversation, and you already know how to do that. I get it. Sometimes it feels like we should already know all of this. In some cases, we do know this intellectually, but we're not sure how to put it into practice. This is an invitation to practice. To figure out how to translate your head knowledge into action. To go from thinking about having a deeper conversation to actually having one. Conversation like this is a skill. It's something a lot of us haven't learned how to do, and so we don't do it. Or we let the people in our life for whom it seems to come naturally be the ones to take the lead, while we simply follow. But if we want to deepen our relationships, if we want to start being present with fewer walls up, we first have to figure out how to have conversations about real things. We have to be willing to share not only facts but also feelings. It's not enough to tell your friends what you did all week if you can't also tell them a bit about what it meant to you.

If we want the world to change, we have to do it together. No more myth of the solitary man. No more John Waynes. We have to do this work in community.

CHAPTER TEN

God-Ordained Masculinity

The messages I received from my religious community about men and what it meant to be a man were that men were to be the leaders. They were the ones who were ordained by God to lead countries and churches and families.

Men were to be the spiritual guides and heads of their communities. But men were also fragile. They could be led to lust by women in spaghetti strap tank tops or two-piece bathing suits. Women were supposed to protect them with modesty. (But I also remember hearing that boys were so unable to control their sexual urges and were turned on by the slightest things that even *linoleum* could lead them to impure thoughts . . . so maybe women couldn't protect them?)

Men were fierce warriors. Men needed to have their hearts tended. Men would fly off the handle, but that's because they weren't being treated right. Men were in charge of their emotions until they weren't. It was a mess of messages.

Growing up, I had a pretty complicated conception of masculinity. On the one hand, I didn't have access to my father. I lived with my mother, grandmother, and grandfather. I was cared for primarily by women: my mother, grandmother, and even my great-grandmothers. But I do remember days when I would go on the road with my grandfather. He owned his own business and worked sometimes as a delivery driver, taking vanloads of potting soil and plant food (and later, as the business expanded, napkins and paper plates) to grocery stores all over our area.

On those days, I would ride shotgun in the van, and he would tell me stories. We would have long-ranging conversations about theology and the world. He was almost always gentle with me. He only lost his temper with me a couple of times in my life that I can remember, but those times were enough to make me not want to upset him again.

My mother got married when I was five, and suddenly there was a stepfather in the picture. He carried himself with an easy masculinity. People would have considered him a man's man. He worked in construction, watched football and fell asleep on the couch on Sunday afternoons, and hunted on long weekends in the fall and winter. Sure, he cried anytime an animal did something cute or got hurt in movies, but that was just about the only time he showed emotion (and only for animals, never for people). He was rather distant, engaging in activities and sports but not much else. He worked long hours, and with him hunting on the weekends, there were many weeks when I didn't see him at all or only in passing.

He could be strict. He had a lot of opinions about how I should be raised and enforced them often. In his mind, I needed to be disciplined, up early, focused on my schoolwork, in bed at a decent hour. It didn't matter that that wasn't how I was wired (nor did it matter that, since I was homeschooled, the regimented life also wasn't necessary). He believed in lots and lots of chores and didn't understand my love of reading.

We fought often. What I saw in him was a man who really only cared about himself. He expected the family life to orbit around him as he dropped in and out whenever he felt like it. He would disappear from my life for days on end and then come home dropping pronouncements about how things should be and what I should be doing. I remember thinking, *You're not even here. What does it matter?* I probably even said that a couple of times when I was a teenager, which didn't make our relationship better. He and my mother would have screaming matches when they fought. I would go in my room and be so angry at him for speaking to her like that.

In him, I saw a man who expected to run the household even when he wasn't in it or participating. I saw self-centeredness. He would take over the television on Sunday afternoons for football and then immediately fall asleep, but no one was allowed to change the channel. So the television would play while he slept in front of it. It didn't matter if anyone else wanted to watch something.

He was tapped for leadership at our church even though he wasn't fit to be a leader. He was volatile, competitive. I remember junior high dodgeball games where lanky preteens were in danger of getting their heads taken off by a ball he threw, and yet he just kept throwing as hard as he could. On our fall retreats, he would dress head to toe in his hunting camouflage so he could dominate at the capture-the-flag game. He was the sports guy. I never remember having conversations of spiritual depth with him. Those fell to my mother.

This was a pattern in my church, men being asked to lead without any of the skills or emotional maturity to do so. I went on a mission trip in high school. In our orientation packets, boys were assigned a Bible text to prepare a sermon around, and girls were assigned a children's story. I read my assigned story and groaned. It was a little cheesy. Besides, children made me uneasy. It's not that I didn't like them, but they always asked me questions about how I was dressed and if I was a boy or a girl, and then the adults around me got all weird and awkward. But I knew this was my assignment, so I got to work learning it. At orientation, we broke up into small groups to practice, girls with girls, boys with boys. When it was my turn, I launched into my story, and my group laughed. I felt my face get red. "What's the matter?" I asked. "You're doing this weird voice. Just talk normally!" Without realizing it, I had done my best kindergarten teacher impression. Now that they had called it out, it was all I could hear, and I was so self-conscious that I rushed through my story.

Throughout the summer, at each stop, one of the boys would be assigned to preach, and one of the girls would be assigned to do a children's story. I was never once assigned. I didn't say anything about it. Somehow I knew I wasn't very good, and everyone could see it.

The thing was, I was actually quite a good public speaker. I had been doing monologues for years, some of them dramatic, some more storytelling in nature. I was comfortable in front of crowds. I was a leader in my youth group. But very quickly I realized that on this trip, I was not allowed to lead. I was supposed to sit back and be led. No one came right out and said it, but they didn't have to. It was baked into the entire fabric of how the summer was designed.

This is how much of the gender education gets passed on. It's not quite overt, but it's also not subtle. In so many conversations and roundabout ways, we get taught what it means to be a man and what it means to be a woman. Or at least what it means to behave like one.

In this religious world, women are responsible for a lot. Protecting men's purity by covering everything up. Keeping the men faithful. Taking care of and teaching children (but only young children; once they get to a certain age, only men should teach them). Making sure everything runs smoothly. It's never said outright that women belong in the kitchen, but that's definitely where you'll find them. Baking communion bread, preparing the bowls of water for the foot-washing service, and doing the mountains of dishes after any event is done.

Purity never quite made sense to me. Women were supposed to dress modestly so as not to make men stumble, but at the same time, we were constantly told that men are turned on by everything. So there was this dichotomy: dress modestly, but also know that even if you were in a burlap sack, men could still be aroused by you. This modesty conversation was particularly weird for me personally because by all standards of modesty, I was crushing it. I wore baggy pants, and when I wore shorts, they went below my knees. My T-shirts and sweatshirts were oversized. I was definitely modest. And yet because I was dressing "too masculine," it overrode my modesty and became some different kind of sin. It was like they wanted me to be hot but not too hot.

I was somehow subverting the idea of purity by dressing the way I did, but what no one would come out and say is that it was because I was violating gender norms. I was dressing too "masculine," and that somehow threw the whole idea of purity out of whack.

That's how tightly the entire system was wound. That's how fragile it all was. My baggy shorts threatened to bring down the entire edifice.

On the mission trip there was one young man on our team whom the leaders, especially JR and Shelly, were determined to hold up as a model. He was young and attractive. He was charming to be around. But he was also really, really bad at leading. He wasn't a confident public speaker. When he was asked to pray for the team, his prayers came out all jumbled and mumbly. I remember thinking even then, *Good grief, stop trying to make this happen!* But they had decided he was the model. There was something about him that made the leaders believe he was the future of the church. And yet they could look at me and not see the future. They could discount the ways I was a natural leader—the way I was willing to step up, the ease I had in front of others—and say I was unqualified simply because of the sex I was assigned at birth.

It didn't make sense. At the time, I wasn't trying to be a pastor, but I did feel called to lead.

In college, I majored in youth ministry. We were told, often, that women were allowed to take the classes, allowed to get the degree, but not allowed to be youth pastors or ministers. Women were required to stop teaching boys once those boys reached a certain age. In most cases, that was roughly around junior high. In my church growing up, we had women who were senior high leaders, but they answered to the pastor, didn't teach the full group, and then led the small groups of girls. Once boys hit senior high, they were considered men, and so were theoretically not to be taught by women anymore.

I was required to do a summer internship for my program, and I went back to the church I grew up in. Over the course of the summer, I planned a weekend beach retreat and gave the lessons at almost every Bible study time. I coordinated the summer ministry trip, which included all the planning and scheduling as well as creating curriculum for a summer vacation Bible school we were going to lead. At the end of the summer, I created a scrapbook along with a report of everything I did. I was proud of it because it had been an incredibly busy summer, but I made it all work. And I did, in fact, lead and teach over the course of this summer. I led devotions and sessions for all genders and all grades, even the senior high.

When I got back to college, I handed over my scrapbook to the two heads of the program, but they barely looked at it. They asked what I planned to do after college, and I talked about my love of theatre and wanting to use drama as a ministry tool. They launched into a lecture about how I should work with children. I tried to explain that I didn't feel called to work with children, but they insisted. I was standing right in front of them, telling them who I was, and they couldn't see me. They were convinced they knew what was best for me, but it had nothing to do with my skills or my calling. It had everything to do with the gender they assumed me to be. Women teach children. That's what they do. They birth children, and they raise children, and they teach children. But at some point, they are no longer fit to teach once those children become adults.

Months after college, while I was serving a church as a youth pastor, I was helping out at the summer camp I went to as a child. I led praise and worship and taught the kids drama. That year's mission trip group came to put on some puppet shows and do their program, and wouldn't you know it, JR and Shelly were the leaders. As JR stepped off the bus, I felt my stomach clench. Even though he no longer had control over me, I felt the same old fear of his disapproval and punishment.

Later in the afternoon, he pulled me aside to talk. He mentioned a girl on their team who wore Converse sneakers and baggy clothes and told me he didn't have a problem with how she dressed because she had a good attitude (the insinuation being, of course, that I hadn't). He went on to lecture me about how I behaved and ended with, "You just have to understand that you can do anything but be a pastor." The silence hung between us for a moment, and then he asked what I was up to these days. I said, "I'm a youth pastor." I could tell he was surprised, and I felt a bit of glee at getting to tell him what I did. To his credit, he said, "Let me pray for your ministry," and even though I didn't really want his prayers, I said, "That'd be great."

These mixed messages about clothing haunted me. Why did this person on their team wearing guy's clothes get a pass, and I didn't? What was it, exactly, about my attitude that had made them so worried about my clothing? As a young person, I couldn't figure it out. Looking back, I realize there was something deeper under the surface. It wasn't just my clothing. It was my clothing coupled with my close relationships with the young women on my team and the masculine energy I exuded. But we didn't have language to talk about such things.

It might seem strange to talk about "masculine energy," but in that strictly gendered world, I violated the norms simply by trying to be myself. Being myself went beyond just my clothing to how I carried myself.

What I saw in masculinity growing up was a privileging of men who often didn't deserve it. Men who were pushed into positions of power and leadership sometimes without even wanting to be there. Men who expected the world to revolve around them simply because they were men.

Sure, there were some outliers: the gentleness of my grandfather, the youth pastor who encouraged me even though other people thought he shouldn't have, the occasional young man who seemed to push back against gendered stereotypes and try to forge his own way in the world. But for the most part, the hierarchy was set.

I, of course, was excluded from the men's-only spaces. When genders were split, I was sent off with the women because that's where everyone assumed I belonged. But I never felt like I fit in those spaces. I remember feeling awkward, uncomfortable, and out of place. Everyone else seemed to know how to behave and what to do, but I felt like I was floundering. Femininity didn't come easy to me. I didn't know how to hold my body. I didn't know what the rules were.

* * *

Whether or not you consider yourself religious, whether or not you consider yourself explicitly Christian, the reality is that at least in the United States, Christianity, and conservative evangelical Christianity in particular, has had an outsized influence on how we understand gender and particularly masculinity.

From the faith and family movement, to the work of the Promise Keepers, to more militant movements like the ones that spawned the Quiverfull families, these models of what it means to be a man are deeply embedded in our culture.

There's this image held up sometimes about what it is to be a good man. It's to be a father, to be a husband, to marry a woman, to financially provide for your family, to have a house in the suburbs with a couple of kids and a dog, to go to church, and to be civic-minded. You join things and mow the lawn on the weekends. As a man, you have your role, and your wife has her role, and they are very different roles.

Maybe you fight in the military, but even if you don't, you support the troops. You put up an American flag on the Fourth of July. You engage in some kind of male bonding: hunting, playing sports, or, at the very least, watching sports. You work hard, and you expect that when you come home, your kids will be there to greet you at the door, and dinner will be close to being ready to put on the table.

We know that this idyllic picture has never been the reality for the vast majority of families. There have always been families where all the adults worked, or many generations lived under one roof, or couples who chose not to have children (or couldn't have children). We know the reality of living in America—of forming relationships, of finding jobs, of participating in civic life—is a lot more complicated for some men than for others. We can sometimes accept that not every man wants to hunt or deal with sports, that some men like reading books or baking or brewing beer. And yet this image of what it means to be a "good man" persists in many corners of our lives and especially in our media. These images are intertwined with God and country and family.

Which almost always means the Christian God, the United States, and the heterosexual nuclear family.

My faith has always been important to me. I grew up steeped in a conservative version of Christianity, and even though my beliefs have shifted, the Christian tradition still feels like home to me, even if it looks nothing like the tradition I grew up in. Funny how two completely different ways of being can share the same name—much like forms of masculinity.

Whether you're Christian or not (or were and are no longer), ideas of masculinity are heavily influenced by Christianity, at least in the United States. Even those of us who are trying to push back against those ideals are still pushing against something that exists and exerts influence on us.

In order to grapple with masculinity, we have to look at the various forms of understanding coming out of evangelical Christianity. These understandings and teachings permeate so much of our lives, often without us even realizing.

* * *

Promise Keepers was founded in 1990 by Bill McCartney. This was a movement designed to get men reconnected with their families. It was created in response to the fear that too many families were fracturing: too many single mothers, too many absent dads, too many divorces. What was needed was a movement that would ask men to show up for their families.

Promise Keeper rallies took over stadiums as men gathered to sing, pray, and make promises. There are seven promises of the Promise Keepers. A Promise Keeper is committed to (1) honoring Jesus Christ through worship, prayer, and obedience to God's Word in the power of the Holy Spirit; (2) pursuing vital relationships with a few other men, understanding that he needs brothers to help him keep his promises; (3) practicing spiritual, moral, ethical, and sexual purity; (4) building strong marriages and families through love, protection, and biblical values; (5) understanding that Jesus calls him to be His hands and feet, serving others with integrity; he purposely lifts up the leadership of the church and his nation in prayer; (6) reaching beyond any racial, denominational, generational, and cultural barriers to demonstrate the power of biblical unity; (7) influencing his world and being obedient to the Great Commandment and the Great Commission.

There is a lot to unpack here. Let's start with the good: Promise Keepers were designed to break men out of isolation, connecting them to other men to have real conversations about what was going on in their lives. This is a powerful and important ideal. This movement also was committed (at least in word) to connecting men across racial, denominational, and generational divides. This wasn't supposed to be a movement just for white men or for a particular denomination. The focus of this group was on helping men be better husbands and fathers. A laudable goal (even if it also assumed all men would be husbands and fathers and that all men would be heterosexual).

From there, this model, while attempting to be flexible, ends in rigidity. What it looks like to be a Promise Keeper, and thereby a good man, is rigid. You are a Christian and not only a Christian; you are a certain type of Christian (even as it's apparently open to all denominations, this way of understanding how you live out your faith is anchored in Evangelical Christianity). You are heterosexual. You are a father and a husband. You live out your faith and your life in set ways. These assumptions that this is what it means to be a good man overtake the benefits of the organization. Promise Keepers still exists today, but the new leadership has taken it in a distinctly partisan direction. This iteration of Promise Keepers is championing Christian Nationalism above all.

* * *

Then there was *Wild at Heart.* John Eldredge's bestselling book, first published in 2001, was about the perceived crisis facing men and what to do about it. In his estimation, "in the heart of every man is a desperate desire for a battle to fight, an adventure to live, and a beauty to love." There's a lot to critique in *Wild at Heart*, but I do think the impetus that caused Eldredge to write is a disquiet that a lot of men truly feel: a sense of boredom and disconnect. Men feel disconnected from themselves, disconnected from their families. Men pour themselves into work and feel bored there too. Or else work becomes their entire life because it's the only place they feel alive. It's because we don't know how to find meaning for ourselves, in ourselves, because that's rarely been modeled for us.

Eldredge looks to mythology, and instead of finding the deeper meaning, he uncritically pulls out the tropes. Men need adventure. They need to fight. And they need to do all of it to impress (and overpower) women. He tries to soften some of the language, saying that women, too, need to fight for their families, but he goes all in on setting men and women as fundamentally different from each other.

Eldredge's version of the hero's journey makes it shallow. The original idea of the hero's journey, popularized by Joseph Campbell, was about learning to take personal responsibility. It was about facing your wounds and overcoming them and then being of service to your community with the knowledge you've gained. It's not about an epic adventure; it's about emotional maturity. To make it into a simple adventure story misses the whole point. In fact, looking at it in this way keeps men chasing the next high: the next fight, the next person to conquer, the next rush of accomplishment. The reality, though, is that men need to be present in the mundane—in the day-to-day, in the household chores, in caring for the kids, in the hard conversations with their spouse. That's heroic. That's what takes courage. If we were to do that, then we'd see our families transform. Instead, we're out slinging around swords without paying any attention to who's going to get hurt.

Men in churches are given a lot of mixed signals. They are supposed to be leaders and warriors but also scholars and teachers. They are to keep themselves from temptation while also realizing they are men who are easily tempted because "God wired them that way." They are to be warriors for Jesus but also raise their hands in worship and be moved by the music.

And so evangelical churches tell men they are right to be bored in their church services while also telling them if they're not bored, then something must be wrong with them. They provide alternative events for men like MMA fighting for Jesus (a real thing) and giving some men engraved swords and having *Braveheart* watch parties.

Men are supposed to be loving fathers but also righteous warriors. Bored and seeking adventure but also engaged in the everyday. Pure but also filled with lust (but, you know, controlling that lust). Men get all sorts of messages.

And in swoop John Eldredge and organizations like the Promise Keepers to solve the dilemma and make it easy. Clear. Men need a battle to fight and a beauty to love. All men. Regardless of their identities (because in Eldredge's and the Promise Keepers' world, only heterosexuality exists) and regardless of what they might desire for their lives. Men are reduced to this: fighting battles and saving women.

There are a few moments when Eldredge nails the problem: "Men are angry, and we really don't know why"; "This is every man's deepest fear: to be exposed, to be found out, to be discovered as an impostor, and not really a man." He also seems to understand some of the nuance: "A man needs to be tender at times, and a woman will sometimes need to be fierce. But if a man is only tender, we know something is deeply wrong, and if a woman is only fierce, we sense she is not what she was meant to be." But his underlying message throughout the book is that culture (and the church) has confused men. It has spent too much time turning them into "nice guys," and as a result, men are totally checked out. But! If they had an epic battle to fight, then maybe they would come alive again.

Eldredge spends a lot of time talking about the camping, wilderness, and rock climbing trips he goes on with his sons. He talks about finding the untamed parts of your heart and the wildness. There is this sense that if men just got outside more, they could bring back some of the fierceness they've been missing. It's not that his ideas about nature are bad; in fact, studies are showing that all of us would be better off if we got outside more often. But Eldredge pushes this sense of adventure only for men and frames it in such a way as to be about violence and domination.

All in all, it feels like "playing battle" more than actually facing a battle. It feels like an attempted return to some kind of made-up American wildness that never really existed in the first place. And more than anything, it prescribes a flat masculinity. One that looks and feels the same for all men everywhere. *Wild at Heart* doesn't have room for the artist or the scholar. It doesn't have room for the stay-at-home dad or the kindergarten teacher. In fact, his acknowledgment that many men worry they will be found to be impostors and considered "not really a man" is steamrolled over by his assertion that all men will only find themselves in the wilderness.

I can imagine reading this book, feeling like I'm not living up to my masculine promise, and being made to feel so much worse. (We won't even talk about his added materials in the updated version that promote conversion therapy and the subtle slights about "gender confusion" throughout the book.)

And yet there is something here, something pulsing under the conflicting messages in this book: Men aren't sure what makes them special anymore. Men aren't sure what makes them *men*.

For so long, men have known where they stand. They are the leaders, the providers, the top of the pecking order. Men are the ones with power and privilege. Men are on the top rung of the ladder. Men do things, and they win things, and they lead things. And now men don't seem to be winning as much. Men don't seem to be leading as much. If women can do all of the things men used to exclusively do, where do men fit? What makes us special? Why are we even here? Men don't seem to know what to do with ourselves.

It seems that for many men, our identities have always been defined by what we are not, and the primacy of what we are not has been simple: we are not women. But now if women can do whatever men can do, what is it that makes us men? How are we different? How are we special? So unspool the narratives about battles and wildness and wilderness. We are meant for anywhere other than here. We are meant for power. We are meant for violence. We are meant to be untamed.

And so, in many ways, Eldredge's solution (similar to Jordan Peterson's) is to throw the blame on women and encourage men to find themselves in the wild.

Eldredge believes that everything is a battle. The cosmic battle between good and evil, the battle between wildness and gentleness, the battle between countries and people. And men's place is to be in the middle of the battle. He never questions if the battle is the right metaphor. If maybe, just maybe, the battle is where it all went wrong in the first place, that it's not about always fighting but instead about finding a way to be in harmony. Peace is never the goal in his world, just more fighting. If men don't have something to fight against, the thinking goes, then they are simply domesticated. They lose their specialness. They become "feminized." Eldredge assumes there will never be peace. His vision is self-perpetuating. If men are always and forever chasing a battle to fight in order to prove their masculinity, then of course there will never be peace!

Instead of dealing with the more fundamental question of what it means to be a man in a changing world, Eldredge instead looks to unchange the world. He wants to put the toothpaste back into the tube. Take us back to the good old days when there were clear wars to fight and evils to banish and men dying in trenches far away from home. It doesn't matter that the world would be better if there were no wars. In his mind, there will always be wars, especially if men are in charge . . . which they should be.

Eldredge (and many others like him) use this doublespeak to back us all into a corner. He doesn't ask, "Is this how we really want to be? Is this actually good for us? Is this leading us to deeper connection and health?" Instead, he and others try to recreate a past that never was. A past where they feel like they will be given the respect they deserve. A past where they'll have all the adventures they long for, and those adventures will give them meaning.

So many white men, in particular, seem to believe if we could just get "back there," then everything will be okay. In their minds, the past is some idyllic land where rules were clear, people knew their place, and everything made sense. They ignore the fact that "back there" means women as objects with no autonomy or protections. "Back there" means slavery and Jim Crow laws and segregation. "Back there" means dangerous jobs with no regulation. It's clinging to a perfect past that was never actually perfect. But what it gave white men was a sense of superiority and power, and if we're being honest, that's what many of these men are trying to return to: a time when they were at the top.

This sense of losing control, of losing power, of losing clarity is why so many men are floundering.

What's underneath all the Evangelical teachings about masculinity is a set of beliefs about power. Who should have it and who shouldn't. Men (but only cisgender heterosexual men and, honestly, mostly only white cisgender heterosexual men) should have it. No one else should. Men rule over their wives and their children. They rule over their churches and their states and their country. They rule. They say that's the nature of things. That's how it was meant to be, but really they created the system.

While there are some men who do want to double down on power and ruling over others, there are other men who hear these teachings and realize something is amiss.

These teachings about masculinity, while they seem to be designed to uphold order and balance, actually end up failing everyone. Men are taught to lead (even if they're not leaders). They are taught to rule over their families. They are taught to be spiritual guides. To be strict with discipline (of both their wives and their children). They are taught to be strong and brave and fight the battles against all sorts of enemies. They are taught to respect their wives but also to lead them. They are taught, of course, that they are heterosexual. They are taught to uphold purity culture but also that they are seconds away from sexual addiction if they watch even one minute of pornography.

When they inevitably fail at any one of these standards, they are told not only are they at risk, but so is their entire family and society. If they fail, they are wretched sinners and at risk of hell. So men try to measure up. They try to follow the rules. They try to do all of the things and then wonder why they're unhappy. They wonder why their kids are afraid of them. They wonder why they don't feel the way they're supposed to feel.

Their church tells them if they don't feel good, then they're not trying hard enough, or they're slipping into sin. So they try even harder. They push more. They rule more. They wonder why they don't feel close to their wife and why they are fighting all the time. They wonder why sex isn't as good as it was promised to be. But they can't talk about this to anyone because every time they try to let someone in, they're confronted for their sin and doubt. They push down their feelings; they don't talk about them. They just keep going.

So many men are trapped in a system that is destroying them and told that feeling bad about it is their own fault because they are broken. Anyone who's in this system who isn't heterosexual, who doesn't want to be a leader, who longs for a more equal relationship with their spouse, who actually cares about their wife's pleasure and well-being, who wants a more tender relationship with their children is going to be made to feel like a failure.

The Evangelical system is particularly concerned about sexuality. While many people are talking about the harms of purity culture on women, we're just beginning to talk about the damage that's been done to men as well. Men are continually given conflicting information. Men are responsible for being pure and protecting the purity of their wives but are also told that without God's help, they are at risk of being driven mad by their sexual urges. The number of sermons I heard in high school from men saying that without God, they would be sex-crazed rapists is more than I can count. This idea that a strong belief in God is the only thing keeping men from ravaging everyone around them makes men question their every thought and emotion.

This emphasis on sexual purity, with every stray thought being considered deeply sinful, makes even natural sexual development feel fraught. If you're told that every single time you think about attraction or sex, it's sin and you're lusting after someone, you become obsessed with cataloging and controlling your thoughts.

Men are given no information about women's bodies and women's pleasure. Sex is supposed to bring them closer to their wife, but also it's for procreation. Women aren't spoken of as people with sexual needs and desires; pleasure is focused on men, and it's women's responsibility to meet their husband's desires. In some Evangelical communities, women are taught they should not (and sometimes cannot) say no to having sex with their husbands. They are to do their Christian duty and meet their husband's sexual needs. This leads to coercive sex, sexual violence, a buildup of resentment, and sexual dysfunction. Sometimes men might not even know how to ask for consent because they've never been taught they need to. Women are taught if they don't have sex, their husbands will cheat on them or leave them.

Men, then, are left feeling like they should have a super-high sex drive, that something is wrong with them if they don't want to have sex all the time. They're also taught that they can't masturbate, thus putting the ability to take care of their own sexual needs (if their wife is uninterested) off the table.

Men in this world are constantly told they are in a battle for the very soul of the nation, and then we wonder why they spend all their time on edge and ready to fight.

Of course, all of this also leads to compulsory hetero-sexuality, where men can't even entertain the idea that they might be attracted to other men. If they do feel same-gender desire, they are often forced to sublimate it or feel they will have to choose between their faith and their ability to be themselves.

There is no space in this world for people who exist outside of the gender binary, there is no room for transgender people, and still gay and lesbian people are told to either sublimate their desires or be celibate.

Again, these ideas permeate even nonreligious spaces. From abstinence-only sex education in many states to ideas about the "proper order" of families, men are being influenced by these notions whether they are part of churches or not.

Baked into all of this is an idea of power and hierarchy, and it's men's job to preserve that power and hierarchy at all costs. Underneath all these teachings is an idea that God is the head of everything and has ordained men to be the head on earth. If men aren't the head, then everything falls apart. Every ill in society is blamed on men not being in their proper place.

For many men, letting go of this idea of power and hierarchy is hard. It makes us feel like we're not sure what we're supposed to be. If we're not in charge, then what are we? If we're not the head of the household, then what role do we have in our family?

Letting go of our ideas of power is one of the hardest things a lot of us will have to do, but it's also one of the most freeing. For a lot of us, this shift in mindset asks us to consider what we might have to give up, but instead I want to ask what you might gain.

What if you didn't have to be in charge all the time? What if you didn't need to have all the answers? What if you didn't need to be the strongest person in the room? What if you could let your guard down, just for a bit?

Can you feel your shoulders relaxing? Can you feel yourself unclenching a bit? What if you could be in community with the people around you instead of ruling over them? What if you could figure it out together?

Trying to always be in charge means being hyperaware, all the time, of where your power is in relation to other people. It means doing everything you can to defend yourself and your position. It means fighting, constantly, to stay at the top. Isn't it exhausting, especially when you're locked in that struggle with the people closest to you? Your spouse and children. Your friends. Shifting to collaboration instead of competition will make all your relationships healthier.

It will also start to alleviate so many of the systemic injustices that plague our country and the world. If we cared less about power and who was on top, we could actually begin to address things like systemic racism, the wage gap, the lack of economic stability, and on and on. But if we remain simply out for power, then we'll never be able to fully overcome these issues.

What does this look like on an individual level? Pay attention to the places where you feel like you have to lead. Do you actually, or might you be able to invite other people into the decision-making process? Do you feel like you have to lead your family? What would it look like to create a way forward together instead?

Freeing ourselves from notions of masculinity that no longer serve us can be difficult, especially with how deeply they are embedded into our culture, sometimes without us even knowing. Paying attention to where these ideas come from, how they've gotten handed down, and why they were espoused in the first place is a helpful corrective. It will make it easier for us to dream up new ways of thinking and being that are good for all of us.

CHAPTER ELEVEN

Facing Down Our Entitlement

Sometimes the models we are given as men are unspoken. We can't point to a figure who embodied them because it's so baked into the fabric of how men behave. One of these models is the model of entitlement.

"Wait a second," I hear you say. "Entitlement is just for rich white guys. I've had to work for everything I've ever been given. I'm not entitled!" I get it. The idea of entitlement makes us think of nepo babies, people who take over their parents' massive corporations, and Ivy League legacy students. Thinking about entitlement in this narrow of a definition serves to let a lot of us off the hook. Let's broaden the definition by asking two questions: What is expected of us? What do we expect of others?

Many of us have been handed a model of masculinity that tells us we're entitled to certain things simply by virtue of our masculinity. We're entitled to sex. We're entitled to houses that are kept up and food on the table. We're entitled to promotions and pay raises. We might not even realize we feel entitled; we just have a sense that this is the way things are. After you work a job for a certain period of time, you get a raise or a promotion, for instance.

I had a much different experience as a child. I was expected to help out around the house. From at least early middle school, I was doing not only my own laundry but laundry for the family as well. I was expected to keep my own room clean, to help with the dishes, and to contribute to yard work. The expectation was since I was part of the family, I contributed to the upkeep of the house and family. When I went on a mission trip in high school, we did laundry once a week, and I remember the women were expected to help out the men. It was an expectation that men either didn't know how to do laundry or shouldn't be responsible for it because they were men. I remember being shocked when I got to college and had classmates who had no idea how to work a washer and dryer. It showed me there were certain things men expected to be done for them. Their laundry would be taken care of without them ever having to touch it.

I didn't realize how gendered some of these things were until I inadvertently messed up. Once, early in my transition, I was at someone's house with my then-wife. We were all playing *Dance, Dance, Revolution*. I was taking a quick break before my next turn, and I turned to my partner and asked if she would get me a glass of water. She went and got the glass of water, but then she lit into me for asking. She said her sister had pulled her aside and said, "Are you going to let him ask you to get him things?" I was upset. I was upset that I had hurt her, but I was also upset that she was reading something gendered into my ask. We fought about it in the car on the way home. I was feeling ashamed, but I didn't know how to say that to her, so instead I told her that if she didn't want to get me the water, she should have just said no. Looking back at that interaction, there's a lot I could have done differently. I could have realized that my asking for the glass of water *was* now gendered because of my gender. I could no longer ask a question like that without the history of gender imbalance reflecting on it. Is that fair? No. Is it reality? Yup. Instead of reacting with anger, I could have told her I was hurt by her response and that I felt shame that she had confronted me in front of her family (which would have been the truth).

What I wasn't yet understanding about my own transition, about my own entry into masculinity and manhood, was there was the weight of an entire history of gendered expectations that I didn't have and wasn't used to. For me, I was the same person I'd always been. I was a person asking another person for a glass of water. But in that moment, that's not how it all played out. Instead, it looked like I was a man asking a woman to get me a drink and asking it in front of other people with the assumption that my partner would get it for me. It triggered all my partner's fears about what it would be like to be married to a man (something she hadn't expected or wanted), about what it meant to move through the world as a straight couple, about the expectations on her.

In that moment, I didn't feel entitled to the drink or to having her get it for me. I didn't even think about it that deeply, but the reactions of both her and her sister showed me I should have. I offer this story to illustrate the ways in which we might not even understand how our actions are affecting the women in our lives. We often don't think we're being entitled because we're not thinking about it at all. Sometimes it's just a genuine oversight (like my asking for the water), and other times it's the messages we've internalized that tell us "this is just the way it is."

Talking about entitlement is often uncomfortable (and sometimes complicated), but if we can confront these feelings and behaviors, we'll do more to change our lives and our relationships than almost anything else.

Maybe you grew up in a household where your mom did all the household stuff, and your dad did all the financial stuff. Maybe you are used to watching television shows where the dad handles their kids' sports activities, and the mom handles school. Maybe you're used to hearing stories about how men pay for the first date and hold doors, and because they do those things, they're more likely to have sex on that date (or at least after the next few). All these messages tell us we're entitled to certain things in life and especially in relationships.

Often, we don't even think about it, nor do we talk about it. Many of us don't go around demanding our partners cook us dinner or clean up the dishes or do the laundry. Many of us don't tell them the kids are their responsibility, and we'll help as needed. We don't tell the women we date that because we paid for dinner, we expect them to have sex with us, but often we carry those unconscious assumptions with us. And because we're carrying those assumptions, we sometimes act like it's a done deal, and so we behave as if we're entitled to those things: a home-cooked dinner, a clean house, time away from the kids, regular sex, whatever it is.

While gay and trans men might not have the same imbalances, we are not immune to experiencing feelings of entitlement. Men expect that people will listen to us when we speak, and they'll respect our ideas and our opinions. We expect we'll get paid at the top level of our range, and we'll get the jobs we apply for. We expect we'll be picked to lead. And yes, some of these things are more expected by cisgender white men because men of color and transgender men know the systems aren't set up to treat them the same way. But even men with more marginalized identities often expect things of the women in their lives.

This sense of being entitled to things causes us to react with anger when things don't go our way. In her memoir *You Could Make This Place Beautiful*, the poet Maggie Smith talks about all the unspoken assumptions in her marriage. Her husband's work was considered the "real work" because it happened out of the house and in an office. His work travel was considered expected, while her work travel was considered "extra" or, even worse, an inconvenience. She was expected to take care of the house since she was home (even though she was *working* from home), and the kids were her responsibility. She writes: "In my marriage, I felt that I needed permission, authorization, to clock out, log off, hand the work to someone else for a few days. 'Can you cover for me?' suggests it is your work to do, not a shared responsibility. I could quote my friend Jen, who says the work she does makes her husband's life possible. I could talk about invisible labor—how there are gears turning inside the machine that no one sees, but if they stop turning the whole thing grinds to a smoking halt." After her divorce, she writes,

> I wasn't good at being the version of myself I needed to be in my marriage. I wasn't good at handling what was, apparently, "the deal." Was the deal that we'd both freeze at the instant of "I do" and not grow or change or succeed or fail or suffer or triumph from that day forward, till death do us part? Or was the deal that he could grow and change, choosing a new career entirely, an incredibly demanding career, and that I would have to put my own dreams on hold because I made less money? Was that the deal?

He felt entitled to her labor at home. He felt entitled to her attention and care. He felt entitled to her not working. That sense of entitlement fractured their marriage.

Entitlement fractures relationships all the time, not just romantic ones but also work relationships, community relationships, and more. When we feel entitled to something, we don't stop to ask how the other person is feeling about it. We don't stop to ask if it's the way things should be structured.

Sometimes our sense of entitlement might be rooted in a feeling of burdensome male responsibility. We feel entitled to a clean home and dinner because we feel responsible for paying the bills and buying the home. We feel entitled to being listened to and cared for by women who are our friends because we feel responsible for shouldering the emotional burden and remaining stoic with our romantic partners. We feel entitled to sex or physical affection because we feel the responsibility to pay for the dates and make them special. But do we really need to shoulder these responsibilities? As we question men's entitlement, we can also question men's so-called responsibilities—the responsibility to lead, to earn, to be strong.

Instead of questioning our entitlement and feelings of responsibility, we often don't talk with our partners about these expectations. It all persists as unexamined assumptions.

* * *

One of the other ways entitlement shows up is in physical space: who takes it up, who feels like they're entitled to it, and who feels like there isn't any for them.

I think of a time when my wife and I visited a restaurant in our town. It's a place with a pub feel. A large bar takes up the center, lots of tables around the space. This is a small town; there are not a lot of places to eat out, and so even though this would maybe, in other places, be called a bar, here it's a restaurant. For dinner on a weeknight, it's a pretty eclectic crew. On Fridays, a musician plays live music: popular songs like "Don't Stop Believing" and "Margaritaville." When my wife and I were there, we tucked ourselves into a booth in back. There was a guy making a lot of noise. Talking loudly, cheering at things. Then when the musician started playing, this guy was yelling between songs. The sound took up the whole place. He wasn't belligerent exactly, not combative, but definitely trying to be the center of attention. He felt no compunction about interrupting every single other person in the restaurant, nor about being rude to the musician. It didn't seem like he was drunk. He was just loud.

This man felt entitled to the space. He felt entitled to being loud, to being focused on, to being heard. I have no doubt that if someone went up to him and tried to quiet him down, he would escalate the situation—"I'm just trying to have a good time! Lay off!"—ignoring the fact that everyone else in this place was *also* trying to have a good time. They were trying to be with their friends or their spouse. They were trying to have conversations or watch the game. They were trying to be in a space without having to think about everyone else.

Or consider the man who sits in the center seat on an airplane and makes sure to take up both armrests and doesn't seem to care that his elbow is digging into your side. Or the guy on the subway who sits with his legs wide open, pushing into the legs of the people next to him or taking up two seats on a crowded car.

You might wonder, *What's the big deal? It's just a little bit of extra room.* But it's about more than just space. It's about entitlement, of feeling like you can do whatever you want no matter how it affects other people. Entitlement says both the armrests are yours. Entitlement says you can touch other people without their consent. Entitlement says you can be as loud as you want at the pub even if no one else is being loud or it interrupts the musician. Entitlement says all public space is your space.

It's also about not paying attention to other people. Since you feel entitled to the space or to being loud, you're not thinking about who you're sharing space with. You don't think about the table next to yours that can't hear each other in conversation because you're yelling. You don't think about the woman whose leg your leg is up against and how uncomfortable she might be feeling. You don't think about the person you might be inconveniencing by having your elbow hanging over the armrest. Because of your entitlement, the people around you suffer.

Most white, straight, cisgender men don't think about any of this because they've never had to. Some men, particularly Black men, also know they are not entitled to the same things white men are. A Black man who did the same thing in the pub that the white man did would most likely have been escorted out or had the police called on him. Black men know they cannot expect to be treated with respect by police officers or security guards. They know they can't take up the same amount of space in public because they might lose their life over it. Think of the reports of Black men being met with violence or police intervention for doing things like jogging, watching birds in the park, or walking home at night.

As someone who grew up assumed female, I received much different messages about how to behave in public space. I was supposed to always be aware of the people around me. If someone moved toward me, I was supposed to get out of the way so they could go around. If I bumped into someone, I was told to apologize.

I learned how to not take up space. To shrink myself down in my seat so that the person next to me could have more space. I learned to speak quietly (if at all) and to make sure everyone else got the chance to share their ideas too.

Women in particular, but also other people who are taught to experience the world differently, learn very quickly what they are not entitled to. They learn what they cannot take for granted. They can't expect safety while walking at night. They can't expect a man to take "no" or "I'm not interested" for an answer without the potential of violence or escalation. They cannot take for granted that they can take a rideshare without being at risk. Women have learned they are not entitled to safety in public spaces. But they should be. And they could be if men were also taught how to behave in public in ways that would put women at ease.

If you want to be a good man, if you want to inhabit your masculinity in a nontoxic way, one of the first things you can do is pay attention to the space you take up and the things you think you're entitled to.

You might want to write this off as just something toxic men do, or as people trying to take away your fun and outgoing personality, or the killjoy of feminism trying to neuter men and make them small. To say that men should consider the space they take up, to consider their entitlement, to focus on how to change with the world is considered an attack on men and masculinity.

Owen Strachan, in his book *The War on Men*, says, "In such a vicious climate, some men lash out, but many simply disappear. They retreat to the basement, to the garage, to the local bar, to video games for hour after hour after hour, to sports and lesser pursuits. Their avocations become their vocations; their hobbies become their life's center." And while his initial comment feels in agreement with the arguments in this book, this is part of Strachan's larger point that feminism is to blame for men's problems. He says, "In a late-feminist age, three of the most common phrases we hear deployed against manhood are these: 'Smash the patriarchy,' 'men are toxic,' and 'the future is female.'" Later he goes on, "The future is a key focus of the enemies of men. The stakes are high in this game. Though woke feminism scorches the masculine penchant for risk-taking, this same movement is taking a considerable risk indeed. It dares to dream of a future that is not male and that, in fact, has precious little place for men in the days ahead. But this is a future that is no future at all." It's women's fault that men feel disengaged. The solution is to get back to the "strong man," where men are allowed to be men—aggressive, risk-takers, leaders—and everything will be okay again. In Strachan's view, it's not that the world has changed, and men have either struggled or outright refused to keep up; it's that the world has changed, and so we need to change it back.

We can certainly look at structural struggles in education and the workforce and make plans for changing those systems. But the solution isn't to blame feminism and drop out. The solution is for us, as men, to figure out what it means for us to exist in this new world. How do we nurture our own resilience? How do we find our worth in other things?

For too long, many men put their worth in their work, in the pursuit of women, in being able to be in charge and dominant. In a world where those behaviors are less lauded, instead of finding new ways to center ourselves, many of us have decided to just stop trying. Or to go even harder into work and trying to impress women.

Instead of placing our value on things outside of ourselves— our work, our romantic conquests, the things we can buy— what if we instead looked to things of more substance? If we looked to our personal development, the quality of our friendships and partnerships, the contributions we make to our neighborhoods and to causes we care about? If we shifted our perspective from "what can I get" to "what can I give"?

Here are some questions you might ask yourself: What do you expect to be done for you? What do you feel you deserve simply for existing? Do you feel other people deserve the same things? What things happen in your household that you don't ever even have to think about? Have you ever had conversations with your spouse, partner, or roommates about those things, or did you just assume that was the way it was done?

What expectations do you have of the women in your life, not just romantic partners but your mother or your coworkers or your friends? Do you go to them when you have emotional stuff that you want to talk about? Do you assume your mom will host holidays or the women in your workplace will organize the birthday celebrations and holiday potlucks? Do you assume the laundry will just get done and dinner will appear on the table and the kids will get put to bed?

How do we unlearn behavior that no longer serves us, especially if we don't really feel like it's not serving us? We know that not knowing how to do things around the house puts more pressure on our partner and makes them unhappy with us, but the feeling of not doing things around the house is one we might actually enjoy especially because, in our experience, things always get done even if we're not the ones doing them. So it feels, in a lot of ways, like this system works for us. Even if we intellectually know it doesn't and we want to change it, it can be hard to override our habits, especially when those habits seem to be working out for us.

The first step is to simply pay attention. Watch how your partner cares for the house. Pay attention to what you do when you get home. Do you immediately flop on the couch? Do you drop your stuff in the hallway where everyone else has to go around it?

How about even before you get home? Do you check in with your partner to see if anything is needed while you're still out?

What about the assumptions you make? Do you simply assume your partner will make dinner for the family? Is that something that just happens, or have you talked about it and made intentional decisions that work for your household? If your partner is doing the cooking, are you helping with the meal planning and shopping? How about the cleanup? What about packing up things for lunches or for leftovers later in the week? How does that work get done, and how involved in that work are you?

How do you show up in your friendships? Do you reach out to people and check in on them? Do you set up the plans to make sure you get to hang out?

Are you giving back to your community? This could look like volunteering for a cause you care about or organizing a neighborhood barbecue or cornhole tournament. You might consider cleaning up the local park or organizing to get a new playground built in your community. Look around and see what's missing or broken and consider how you might be able to contribute to making it better.

Once you've spent some time with these questions and really answered them honestly, the next step might be to have a conversation with some of the women in your life. You might talk with your partner about how you're separating household chores and responsibilities. You might offer to take on planning the office holiday events. You might make more space for your friends to share what's going on in their emotional lives instead of assuming they have other people to talk to.

You might ask your partner what they've felt you assumed would just get taken care of or the places where they've felt you thought you were entitled to things. Be willing to listen with an open mind and heart and not get defensive. It's only when we face our own behavior (and how it's affecting other people) with honesty that we can begin to shift our lives and our relationships.

You might also start to pay attention to the space you're taking up: physically but also emotionally and with your words. At your office meeting, do you talk over the women? Do you cede the floor so they can share their ideas? In a debate, is it always the person who's the loudest that wins (and are you always the loudest)?

What might shift in your life if you take a step back? If you had to pay more attention to how you were holding your body and sitting in your chair? Does it feel uncomfortable (or unfair) to even consider those questions? Now you're beginning to have a sense of what many people around you are experiencing all the time. Use that to build up your empathy and see how your changing behavior might make things easier for other people.

Unlearning entitlement is about considering our part in the larger community. Instead of assuming things will get done, we participate fully. We treat the people around us as equals, also worthy of consideration, of space, of desire, and of agency.

CHAPTER TWELVE

Where We Go from Here

As a transgender man, one of the biggest things I've had to come to terms with is there will always be some people who will simply not believe I am who I say I am. There are people (even people close to me) who will refuse to use the right pronouns for me or understand I am a man. There will be people in the world who think I am sick and deranged. There are those who will do whatever they can to legislate away my right to exist. They will try to make sure I can't access medical care or have protection under the law. While I work to combat these things, I have to face the reality that there are some minds I just won't be able to change. There are some people I won't be able to bring along no matter how hard I try.

Instead of seeing that as a cause for despair or giving up on trying, I instead focus on the people who do want to change.

I focus on the young people who are just coming to terms with their own identities and are looking for role models to follow. I pay attention to building the world I want to live in and leave for those coming after me.

As we draw close to the end of this book, you might be feeling a lot of things. There might be a sense of hope, a sense of fear, and maybe even a bit of despair. After all, we hopefully understand part of the problem now. We've got some ideas on how to start making changes, but the fear is still there. What if we try all of this and it still doesn't work? What if we can't change things? And what about the people who aren't interested in doing the work?

Any time we consider making change in the world, no matter what the issue, at some point what comes up is "But what about the outliers?" Meaning, what about the people who are so committed to the cause we're against? The one's who've been radicalized? How do we reach them?

Whether we're talking about the extreme transphobia of the TERF community, the racism of the Proud Boys, or the misogyny of Andrew Tate and his followers, the question always comes up. To be honest, I'm not entirely sure what the answer is. After over a decade of work in LGBTQ+ religious organizing, what I've learned is that when someone is committed to misunderstanding you, it's pretty damn hard to win them over. What I have seen work, at least in the beginning stages, is to legislate around people's beliefs. When same-gender marriage became legal in the United States, for instance, it didn't matter what people believed about gay marriage because they could no longer discriminate against it. (Of course, we're now seeing the threat of those rights being rolled back and taken away, so we must remain vigilant.) But if we begin by changing culture enough that these extreme beliefs fall far enough out of fashion that it costs the holders of these beliefs something real to continue to hold them, we begin to move the needle forward.

At the outset, we focus less on those most opposed to what we're trying to do. We don't concentrate on converting Matt Walsh or Andrew Tate or Jordan Peterson. We don't try to convince every man on the planet, especially those who are convinced that nothing is wrong and we should just get ourselves back to the '50s, when men were men and women knew their place. No, instead we start where we are: with the guys like us. The ones who sense there could be so much more. The ones who want to change. The ones who long for deeper connections, stronger relationships, and to not feel so at odds with their emotions, their bodies, and in their relationships. It's not about changing every single man; it's about changing enough of us so culture changes. And honestly, it's not even about *changing* us; it's about letting us out of the boxes we're trapped in, freeing us from the ideas that run counter to how we really feel. It's not about learning a new way of being; it's about restoring us to the way we've always felt we really are.

It's about freeing men to be their fullest selves.

But part of this work has to be enough men stepping up, being loud, and speaking boldly about behaving in a new way. We have to be loud enough to drown out the folks who platform (and profit off of) misogyny. We need to be in the places where young men can hear these messages. We need to counter what they're learning from the media, from YouTube, and even from the men around them. It's not enough to just do this work quietly or with our friend groups; if we're really going to make a difference, we need to be public with our work.

Right now, young men and boys are being left to their own devices, and they are finding their models online. They're absorbing an idea of masculinity that is toxic, not only to them but also to everyone around them. These young men are hearing that they need to put women in their place and take what they want. They are being taught that violence and rage are how they should be expressing themselves, that something has been taken from them and they need to take it back by being crude and rude. They are taught to denigrate everyone who's different from them and sit in an entitlement that justifies all their bad behavior. They absorb all of this and call anyone who behaves differently *soft*.

We have to reach them where they live, showing them another way is possible. But before we can even do that work, we have to believe it ourselves. We have to live it out ourselves.

*   *   *

You might wonder, "What happens if I step into a new way of being, and it makes the people in my life mad? What if I am accused of not being the 'right type of man' or not being strong enough or not being manly enough?"

There will always be some folks who won't change, who will refuse to be willing to look at how systems that trap men into little boxes are bad for all of us. There will be people, of all genders, who feel like they benefit from patriarchy and refuse to change. We can't force anyone to change, but we can take ownership and agency over our own lives and make the changes we want to see. At some point, people might come around, but even if they don't, that's not on us. All we can do is our best internal work.

Some of the people who refuse to change will literally get left behind—the ones who refuse to learn new job skills, the ones who wait for the "old ways" to come back, the ones who refuse to pay any attention to a changing world. If we don't want to be one of the ones left behind, we have to be willing to confront the ways in which the world is changing and make peace with the things that aren't coming back.

We have a responsibility to lean into health for ourselves and our communities. We cannot wait until everyone gets on board before we start to do this work. In this final chapter, I want to offer some practical tips for putting the ideas in this book into practice.

GET A FRIEND—YOU CANNOT DO THIS JOURNEY ALONE

You need to have at least one person in your life, another man, who is willing to embark on this project with you. It needs to be a man because many of us have learned to turn to women to help us regulate and process our emotions. When we do that, we can create an imbalance and put more emotional labor on our partners and friends who are women. This doesn't mean you can't talk to the women in your life or process if you have a female partner; in fact, you definitely should! But the bulk of your work needs to be with another man who you are not romantically connected to. Part of what we're trying to do is live into a new kind of masculinity and help other men do the same, so we need to do this in community.

As you look around your friend group, is there a man who comes to mind? Someone who is kind. Who listens. Someone you feel like you can trust. Someone you feel like you can let down your guard with. Someone who is also interested in doing the work to be a different type of man. Start with them.

Maybe you read this book together and talk about it. Or you commit to checking in with one another on a weekly basis about the things you're learning and experiencing. Or you have intentional conversations about how you're feeling and what's really going on in your life.

IDENTIFY WHAT'S NOT WORKING FOR YOU

Taking apart something as large as our culture of masculinity can seem completely overwhelming. You can start to feel like the entire world needs to change, and you have no idea where to even begin. How do you shift your relationships *and* change systemic structures *and* raise your kids differently *and* take care of your heart?

You do it like you do any project: in stages. The first stage is to diagnose the problem. Maybe the biggest issue in your life is feeling like you're not allowed to show any emotion. Maybe it's feeling like you don't know how to contribute to your own household. Maybe you feel like you've got a tough shell on that you want to get rid of. Maybe you're longing to have a friend to have deeper conversations with. Whatever is feeling the most pressing is where you should start. Trust that if you begin to work on one area, others will follow. We start to untangle the knot of masculinity one string at a time, and we trust that if we just keep working on the knot, eventually we'll get it all unraveled.

So what's not working for you?

IDENTIFY WHAT YOU WANT

The flip side of what's not working is to lean into what you *do* want. Do you want closer relationships? More emotional range? Do you want to feel more ease in your body? Do you want more male friendships? Do you want to feel assured in your masculinity? Do you want a better partnership with the person you're in a relationship with? Do you want to be more tender?

This is a place to dream, to think big about what could be. Don't worry about how you're going to make it happen—not yet. Just spend some time thinking about what you really want.

START SMALL

You didn't learn how to be the type of man you are overnight; you're not going to learn how to be a new type of man overnight. Deprogramming ourselves takes time. It takes energy and work. It takes some trial and error. So start small and build up from there. Find one man to talk to. Try one new practice. Interrupt one behavior that's no longer working for you. Learn to identify and name a small set of new emotions.

PUT PRACTICES INTO PLACE THAT SUPPORT YOUR GROWTH

Learning to do new things takes practice, and systems and routines can help us as we learn how to turn them into habits. Here are some of the practices I have found most helpful for me and when I've been coaching other people.

Journaling. Having a place where I don't have to worry about saying it perfectly is super helpful. A place where I can be safe to let out all of my emotions. Journaling also helps me be more aware of what I'm actually feeling (and what's underneath that emotion) and pay attention to patterns in my life.

Meditation. Meditating (even just for a couple of minutes a day) is another way of practicing awareness. It's not about clearing your mind of thoughts; it's about being aware of when your thoughts get loud. Meditating allows things to come to the surface and helps us have a pause between emotion and reaction.

Therapy. Therapy isn't just for when there's an emergency; in fact, therapy can often prevent emergencies. Having an outside person to talk to, one who is neutral and not involved in the situation, can help us make better sense of things. For those of us who have experienced trauma or harsh teachings about masculinity in our families or churches, therapy can help us get clear on how what we experienced is continuing to affect us. If you're in a relationship with a lot of conflict, therapy can also help you have better and clearer conversations with one another and get to the root of what's actually going on.

To-do lists to make sure you're contributing to the household. It's not cheating to have a list. As you're learning to be a better contributor to your household (or learning how to take better care of the place where you live and learn new skills around household tasks), create some lists to help you stay on track. Maybe you make a list of things you need to clean each week or grocery lists for the meals you're going to learn to cook. Maybe you make a list of all the important information you should know about your kids (their doctors and teachers, when they are due for vaccines, etc.).

Regular check-ins with your male friends. Put them on the calendar and show up for them. Come ready to enter into deeper conversations.

Take care of your body. This isn't all just about our emotional life; we also have to take care of our physical selves. This is about more than just fitness or going to the gym. It's even about more than eating better food. We need to go to the doctor on a regular basis. Go to the dentist. Get up to date on your vaccinations. Schedule that colonoscopy or yearly physical. Take the medication that's been prescribed to you.

Practicing being wrong, being uncomfortable, being challenged. We're not always going to get it right. We're going to say things that are wrong. We're going to hurt people. We're going to overstep (or not step up enough). When we're confronted with our bad or harmful behavior, we need to sit with those emotions and deal with them. We need to get comfortable with discomfort. We need to accept correction from the people in our lives without getting defensive or lashing out. (When we're in one of these situations, it helps to rely on our other practices like journaling, meditation, and conversations with friends to help us process the hard emotions.)

Apologize. We need to learn to apologize well and often. It's not saying, "I'm sorry you feel that way." Or "I'm sorry, but if you had just . . ." Learn how to apologize. Learn to understand what you're apologizing for.

Learn. Course-correct. After you've apologized for the harm done, change your behavior. Continue to learn about the ways toxic masculinity, power, hierarchy, control, white supremacy, violence, and all the other myths we've explored in this book are affecting your life and the lives of other people. Listen to women. Listen to people of color. Listen to trans and queer folks. Listen to communities you're not a part of. Learn. And then change your behavior.

This is an ongoing practice. We continue to learn; we continue to iterate. We don't just learn the lesson once and then move on; we continue to learn (and screw up and apologize and revert), and we continue to try. We have to understand how connected it all is. We have to examine all of it. It's not just one thing; it's the entire system. You can't just look at, for instance, talking about or expressing your feelings more; you need to look at the systems that make you and others feel like you weren't allowed to experience or express the full range of emotion. You can't simply look at your personal relationship and do more to help your household without looking at the entire system that assumes men won't help out at home. You can't just free yourself to choose whatever kind of work works for you without asking questions about the nature of work itself and how we gender jobs and what jobs we prioritize and pay well and which ones we don't and how all of that is connected.

The personal work we do—the things we unpack, the behaviors we unlearn, the family structures we create—aren't just for us; they're for society as well. We do this work so we can expand this work to our families and then to our workplaces and our neighborhoods and our cities and our state and on and on. We start with the personal, but we refuse to stop there. We recognize the things that affect us also affect the broader community.

As we continue to do our personal work, the next part of the work is starting conversations with the men in our lives. Instead of being happy with surface conversation, put in the effort to go a bit deeper. You don't have to go all the way to childhood trauma in your first conversation, but you do need to be intentional. Maybe the next time one of your friends relays some information about his family (maybe a sick kid or an overworked partner or a doctor's appointment), instead of just taking in the information, follow up with a question like "How are you feeling about that?" It might seem strange at first (and you might not get much of an answer the first time you ask), but with practice, it will lead to more depth in your conversations and therefore your relationships as well.

Then we also start conversations with the women in our lives. Not to ask them what we should be doing or to get cookies for trying to do the right thing but to open up a dialogue. We need to let the women we love into our journey. This could look like saying something like this to your partner: "Hey, I've been realizing I've been conditioned to only express anger. I'd really like to lean into the full spectrum of my emotions. I feel like that's going to be good for not just me but you as well. But it might also mean that how I react to things looks different. Or I might need to figure out how to have language to express things. I just wanted you to know what's going on with me." It could even be simpler: "I want to do more around the house. From now on, I'll take care of these tasks every week." And then following through.

This is going to take some trial and error. You're going to mess it up. Keep going. You might get pushback. Instead of quitting, use it as an opportunity to open up another conversation and lean into the growth happening. Any time we shift the balance that people are used to, even if it's in a positive direction, it takes some getting used to. If your partner isn't used to you expressing a lot of emotion, or being more engaged with the running of the household, or asking to talk more often, it might make them uneasy at first. They might feel something is wrong or you're unhappy instead of seeing this as a chance for both of you to be more fulfilled. Allow them to have their own experience and realize they might be distrustful, especially if you have a history of making big promises and then not following through. How they respond isn't your work; your work is to do your work and keep showing up.

* * *

We can change the way we've been living. We can break the molds we've been handed that no longer fit us. We can find new ways to be men and create a culture of health, wholeness, and liberation for all people. But first we have to start with ourselves. We have to do our own work. We have to root out the places in our lives where we're harboring notions that are harmful to ourselves and others. We have to root out our hidden shame and bring it to light. We have to let go of our fear of inadequacy and how that makes us inhibit ourselves as we try to measure up to a standard we don't even care about. We have to unlearn our learned incompetence and be contributors to our households and communities. We have to unlearn our anger and violence and tap into a larger well of emotions and expressions. We need to unlearn the tough-guy approach and allow ourselves to be sensitive too. We need to unlearn competition and our hatred of women, rooting out all the ways that misogyny (even casually) poisons our lives and our relationships. We need to unlearn the idea that we can do it all by ourselves and that we don't need anyone else in our lives. We need to unlearn ideas of dominance and separation and instead see ourselves as part of communities, not just here to rule. We need to unlearn our entitlement and instead learn to adapt and grow.

If it sounds like a lot, it is. But we are capable of it. We just have to want it. We have to be willing to put in the work. We have to rise to the challenge. If you're looking for a battle to fight, a mission to be on, a goal to strive for, this is it. It's not outside us; it's within us. We can learn better ways to inhabit our masculinity that lead to wholeness for us and for the people around us.

We get to be intentional about how we inhabit and embody our masculinity. We get to be intentional about how we form our relationships and show up for ourselves and others. This intentionality will free us from ideas, behaviors, and ways of being that are keeping us small and hindering our health and growth.

No one taught us how to be men. No one taught us how to change and grow and be resilient. No one taught us how to thrive in a changing world. But that doesn't mean we can't learn and then teach others.

Let's get started.

Notes

Introduction

3 ***While there haven't been the same well-defined waves:*** Sarah Pruitt, "What Are the Four Waves of Feminism?" History, March 2, 2022, updated October 4, 2023, https://www.history.com/news/feminism-four-waves.

4 ***From men delaying going to the doctor:*** Leah Campbell, "Why So Many Men Avoid Going to the Doctor," Healthline, September 14, 2019, https://www.healthline.com/health-news/why-so-many-men-avoid-doctors#The-dangers-of-avoiding-doctors-.

4 ***to men having few to no friends:*** "Male Loneliness: The Ticking Time Bomb That's Killing Men," accessed June 13, 2024, https://www.happiness.com/magazine/health-body/male-loneliness-time-bomb-killing-men/.

4 ***to the high rates of suicide:*** "Suicide Data and Statistics," U.S. Centers for Disease Control and Prevention, April 25, 2024, https://www.cdc.gov/suicide/suicide-data-statistics.html.

4 ***men are also struggling with how to parent:*** Rachel Minkin and Juliana Menasce Horowitz, "Gender and Parenting," Pew Research Center, January 24, 2023, https://www.pewresearch.org/social-trends/2023/01/24/gender-and-parenting/.

4 ***how to date and find partners:*** Bob Curley, "Why Young Adults, Especially Men, Are Having Sex Less Frequently," Healthline, June 18, 2020, https://www.healthline.com/health-news/young-adults-especially-men-having-sex-less-frequently.

4 ***There are direct links between the ways men:*** James V. P. Check, Daniel Perlman, and Neil M. Malamuth, "Loneuness and Aggressive

Behaviour." *Journal of Social and Personal Relationships* 2, no. 3 (1985): 243–252. https://doi.org/10.1177/0265407585023001.

Chapter 1: Suffering in Silence

14 *Article written by Donna Minkowitz:* Donna Minkowitz, "Love Hurts," *Village Voice*, April 19, 1994, https://www.digitaltransgenderarchive.net/files/tx31qh69s.

14 *Why did I assume this:* Donna Minkowitz, "How I Broke, and Botched, the Brandon Teena Story," *Village Voice*, June 20, 2018, https://www.villagevoice.com/how-i-broke-and-botched-the-brandon-teena-story/.

15 *"I auditioned drag kings":* Jude Dry, "As 'Boys Don't Cry' Joins National Film Registry, Kimberly Peirce Addresses Its Complicated History," IndieWire, December 12, 2019, https://www.indiewire.com/features/general/kimberly-peirce-interview-boys-dont-cry-transgender-1202196536/.

15 *"I want to thank Brandon Teena":* "Academy Awards Acceptance Speech Database," March 26, 2000, https://aaspeechesdb.oscars.org/link/072-3.

18 *"No wonder guys lose it sometimes":* Max Wolf Valerio, *The Testosterone Files: My Hormonal and Social Transformation from Female to Male* (Emeryville, CA: Seal Press, 2006).

Chapter 2: Naming the Wound

34 *One of the first sources:* Robert Bly, *Iron John: A Book about Men* (Reading, MA: Addison-Wesley, 1990).

35 *Bly draws on an idea:* Robert Bly, *Iron John* (Cambridge, MA: Da Capo Press, 2004), 93.

36 *Growing up in a high control religion:* Accessed July 15, 2024, https://dobsonlibrary.com/resource/article/87d9437e-f158-4b16-a81a-63eeac6bf478.

36 *There is the overbearing mother:* Bly, *Iron John* (2004), 135.

Chapter 3: Finding Safety in Our Bodies

60 *Machines pose a greater threat:* Richard V. Reeves, *Of Boys and Men: Why the Modern Male Is Struggling, Why It Matters, and What to Do about It* (Washington, DC: Brookings Institution Press, 2022), 21.

60 *Health care and education are very large sectors:* Reeves, *Of Boys and Men*, 152.
60 *"number of nurses and nurse practitioners needed":* Reeves, *Of Boys and Men*, 154.
60 *Survey conducted at the end of 2021:* Reeves, *Of Boys and Men*, 154.
60 *In schools, too, we're seeing a rise of available jobs:* Reeves, *Of Boys and Men*, 155.
60 *"only 3% of pre-K and kindergarten teachers":* Reeves, *Of Boys and Men*, 163.

Chapter 4: Unlearning Learned Incompetence

64 *"It's too late to do anything about the inequity":* Maggie Smith, *You Could Make This Place Beautiful: A Memoir* (New York: One Signal Publishers/Atria, 2023).
66 *men are from Mars:* John Gray, *Men Are From Mars, Women Are From Venus: A Practical Guide for Improving Communication and Getting What You Want in Your Relationships* (New York: HarperCollins, 1992).
70 *reminding is characterized as nagging:* Eve Rodsky, *Fair Play: A Game-changing Solution for When You Have Too Much to Do (and More Life to Live)* (New York: G.P. Putnam's Sons, 2019), 45.
70 *"Ownership belongs to the person":* Rodsky, *Fair Play*, 45.
71 *She recommends "having a collaborative discussion":* Rodsky, *Fair Play*, 149.
72 *The goal of Fair Play:* Rodsky, *Fair Play*, 119.
76 *men often think:* Lois M. Collins, "Your Husband Thinks He's Doing Equal Housework. You Probably Disagree," September 21, 2020, https://www.deseret.com/indepth/2020/9/21/21438627/american-family-survey-household-labor-division-husband-wife-children-pandemic-afs-2020-byu/; Sirena Bergman, "Almost Half of Men Think Housework Is Shared Equally—But Research Shows Women Disagree," *Independent*, September 10, 2019, https://www.independent.co.uk/life-style/men-women-parenting-housework-childcare-a9098091.html.

Chapter 5: Accessing More Emotions

94 *"It's lauded as 'tradition'":* Andrew Reiner, *Better Boys, Better Men* (San Francisco: Harper One, 2020), 136.

Chapter 6: Tough Guys Don't Win

106 *There were all sorts of "passing" tips: Passing* in the transgender community is a complicated conversation. It's used as a shorthand for being perceived by others as the gender you are trying to be. For many transgender men, especially early in their medical transitions, passing is a fraught thing. If you don't pass, you could be harassed or assaulted. At the same time, there is an insinuation that if someone is trying to pass, they are tricking other people. That's not how this term should be understood.

117 *"Men are overwhelmingly more likely":* Paul J. Fleming et al., "Men's Violence against Women and Men Are Inter-related: Recommendations for Simultaneous Intervention," *Social Science and Medicine* 146 (December 2015): 249–256, https://doi.org/10.1016/j .socscimed.2015.10.021.

Chapter 7: Collaboration over Competition

121 *12 Rules for Life: An Antidote to Chaos Promises a Solution:* Jordan B. Peterson, Doidge Norman, and Ethan Van Scriver, *12 Rules for Life: An Antidote to Chaos* (Toronto: Random House Canada, 2018).

122 *"Walk tall and gaze forthrightly":* Peterson, Norman, and Van Scriver, *12 Rules for Life.*

122 *"You should be a monster":* "Be a Monster in 2023—Jordan Peterson," Motivational Speech, accessed June 13, 2024, https://youtube.com /shorts/ORrepRouHLM?si=kXiSs8GFy1J7yh4g.

Chapter 8: Femininity Is Not the Enemy

136 *Transgender people struggle to find stable housing:* For more, take a look at the National Center for Transgender Equality's 2022 report, https://ustranssurvey.org, as well as the 2011 report "Injustice at Every Turn," https://www.thetaskforce.org/app/uploads/2019/07/ntds_full .pdf.

136 *Add on compounding marginalizations:* "Facts about Suicide among LGBTQ+ Young People," The Trevor Project, January 1, 2024, https://www .thetrevorproject.org/resources/article/facts-about-lgbtq-youth-suicide/.

138 *We see this play out during gender reveals:* https://www.instagram .com/reel/C3i4U57oKtK/?utm_source=ig_web_copy _link&igsh=MzRlODBiNWFlZA==; https://www.tiktok.com/@ matthb92/video/6954951229286010113?is_from_webapp=1&sender _device=pc&web_id=7338596004536682027.

138 *There have been a couple of videos:* https://www.tiktok.com/discover
/man-gets-angry-at-gender-reveal?is_from_webapp=1&sender
_device=pc.

Chapter 9: We Cannot Do This Alone

146 *Reports have started to come out lately:* Daniel A. Cox, "America's "Friendship Recession" Is Weakening Civic Life," Survey Center on American Life, August 24, 2023, https://www.americansurveycenter.org /newsletter/americas-friendship-recession-is-weakening-civic-life/.

146 *"the percentage of men with at least six":* Daniel A. Cox, "American Men Suffer a Friendship Recession," Survey Center on American Life, July 6, 2021, https://www.americansurveycenter.org/commentary /american-men-suffer-a-friendship-recession/.

148 *From the health problems:* Campbell, "Why So Many Men Avoid Going to the Doctor."

148 *to the mental health problems:* "Suicide Data and Statistics."

148 *"Loneliness and social isolation are associated":* Caitlin Pagán, "Why Close Friendships Are Important for Men's Health," Verywell Health, August 10, 2023, https://www.verywellhealth.com/men-close-friendships -7570202#:~:text=Having%20strong%20and%20meaningful %20friendships,challenging%20times%2C"%20he%20said.

151 *On an episode of Deep Questions with Cal Newport:* https://podcasts .apple.com/us/podcast/deep-questions-with-cal-newport/id1515786216 ?i=1000628244999.

Chapter 10: God-Ordained Masculinity

172 *From the faith and family movement:* The term Quiverfull comes from Psalm 127:3–5:

No doubt about it: children are a gift from the Lord; the fruit of the womb is a divine reward. The children born when one is young are like arrows in the hand of a warrior. The person who fills a quiver full with them is truly happy! They won't be ashamed when arguing with their enemies in the gate. (Common English Bible)

It refers to a movement that encourages families to have as many children as possible. These families are against any kind of birth control or even natural family placing. Many families consider having a lot of children to help with increasing the number of Christians in the world.

174 ***There are seven promises of the Promise Keepers:*** "7 Promises of a Promise Keeper," Promise Keepers, accessed June 13, 2024, https://promisekeepers.org/about-us/7-promises/.

176 ***"in the heart of every man":*** John Eldredge, *Wild at Heart: Discovering the Secret of a Man's Soul* (Nashville: Thomas Nelson, 2021), 8.

178 ***"Men are angry":*** Eldredge, *Wild at Heart*, 40.

178 ***"This is every man's deepest fear":*** Eldredge, *Wild at Heart*, 42.

178 ***But if a man is only tender:*** Eldredge, *Wild at Heart*, 36.

179 ***studies are showing that all of us would be better off:*** David G. Pearson and Tony Craig, "The Great Outdoors? Exploring the Mental Health Benefits of Natural Environments," *Frontiers in Psychology* 5 (2014): 1178, https://doi.org/10.3389/fpsyg.2014.01178.

Chapter 11: Facing Down Our Entitlement

194 ***"In my marriage, I felt that I needed permission":*** Smith, *You Could Make This Place Beautiful*, 102–103.

194 ***I wasn't good at being the version of myself:*** Smith, *You Could Make This Place Beautiful*.

199 ***"In such a vicious climate":*** Owen Strachan, *The War on Men: Why Society Hates Them and Why We Need Them* (Washington, DC: Salem Books, 2023), 50–51.

199 ***"Smash the patriarchy":*** Strachan, *The War on Men*, 18.

199 ***"men are toxic":*** Strachan, *The War on Men*, 20.

199 ***"the future is female":*** Strachan, *The War on Men*, 23.

199 ***"The future is a key focus of the enemies of men":*** Strachan, *The War on Men*, 25, 26.

199 ***The solution is to get back:*** Strachan, *The War on Men*, xxxi.